Lump Sum Mortgage Payoff Secrets

How to Use Bonuses, Side Income, and Windfalls to Eliminate Your Mortgage Faster

By Joseph G. Correa

Copyright & Legal Notice

Published by Live Stronger Faster

First Edition, 2026

Table of Contents

Introduction

For most homeowners, the mortgage becomes one of the largest and longest financial commitments they will ever carry. A traditional 30-year mortgage may appear manageable because of its monthly payment structure, but what many borrowers fail to realize is that the true cost of a mortgage is not simply the home price—it is the decades of accumulated interest that quietly drains wealth over time. Many people spend hundreds of thousands of dollars in interest without ever fully understanding how dramatically they could reduce those costs through strategic principal reduction. The good news is that paying off a mortgage early does not always require extreme sacrifice, impossible budgeting, or doubling every monthly payment. In many cases, the fastest path to mortgage freedom comes from something far more powerful: strategic lump sum payments.

Lump sum mortgage payoff strategies are among the most overlooked wealth-building tools available to homeowners. While most borrowers focus only on making minimum monthly payments, financially intelligent homeowners understand that even occasional large principal reductions can completely transform the life of a loan. A single bonus from work, a tax refund, a business windfall, commission income, inheritance money, investment gain, side hustle profit, or real estate cash flow can potentially eliminate years from a mortgage and save tens or even hundreds of thousands of dollars in future interest. The key is understanding how to use these lump sums strategically rather than emotionally.

Many people receive periods of increased income throughout their lives. Some receive annual bonuses. Others earn commissions, profit distributions, overtime income, or seasonal revenue. Entrepreneurs may experience strong months in business. Real estate investors may generate unexpected profits from property sales or refinancing. Families may receive inheritances, legal settlements, gifts, or investment gains. Unfortunately, many individuals spend these financial opportunities without fully understanding the long-term impact that a properly applied lump sum payment could create. Instead of using a windfall to buy temporary lifestyle upgrades, they could use part of that money to permanently reduce debt, lower financial stress, increase future cash flow, and accelerate wealth creation.

This book is designed to help you understand the psychology, mathematics, and strategy behind using lump sum payments to eliminate mortgage debt faster while maintaining long-term financial flexibility. The goal is not to encourage reckless payoff behavior or to convince every homeowner to throw all available cash into their mortgage immediately. Instead, this book teaches balance, strategy, and intelligent decision-making. There are situations where aggressive payoff makes sense, and there are situations where liquidity, investing, or business expansion may create greater long-term benefits. Understanding the difference is critical.

One of the most powerful realities about mortgage payoff is that principal reductions create permanent financial improvements. Unlike many expenses that temporarily improve lifestyle but disappear quickly, a principal reduction permanently lowers the interest charged over the remaining life of the loan. This means every dollar applied strategically toward principal has the potential to create a compounding financial benefit. When large lump sums are applied early in a mortgage, the results can be dramatic because mortgages are heavily front-loaded with interest during the early years. By reducing principal aggressively during these periods, borrowers interrupt the lender's interest schedule and reclaim wealth that would otherwise be lost over decades.

Many homeowners are shocked when they first see the mathematics behind mortgage amortization. During the first several years of a 30-year mortgage, a large portion of every payment goes toward interest rather than principal. This means borrowers may feel like they are making progress while their loan balance decreases slowly. Strategic lump sum payments directly attack this imbalance. Instead of waiting years for normal amortization to gradually reduce the balance, lump sums accelerate equity growth immediately. The borrower gains ownership in the property faster, reduces future interest obligations, and increases long-term financial security.

What many homeowners fail to understand is that reducing the principal balance early changes the entire trajectory of the loan. Even modest reductions can dramatically reduce total interest because interest calculations are based on the remaining unpaid balance. Every principal reduction weakens the lender's ability to collect future interest from the borrower.

Another important concept discussed throughout this book is the difference between emotional spending and strategic wealth building. Many individuals experience financial breakthroughs but fail to improve their long-term position because they increase lifestyle spending every time income rises. A larger tax refund becomes a vacation. A work bonus becomes a luxury purchase. Business profits become lifestyle inflation. Over time, income rises but long-term wealth remains stagnant because increased earnings are constantly consumed rather than redirected toward asset growth or debt reduction. Financially disciplined individuals behave differently. They intentionally allocate portions of unexpected income toward permanent financial improvements that strengthen future stability.

This does not mean life should become joyless or restrictive. In fact, strategic lump sum mortgage payoff can increase future freedom and reduce stress dramatically. Many homeowners feel trapped by monthly obligations. Mortgage debt often influences career decisions, investment risk tolerance, retirement planning, and overall peace of mind. The faster a homeowner reduces debt, the more flexibility they create in nearly every area of life. Lower debt often means greater career freedom, increased investment options, earlier retirement opportunities, stronger emergency preparedness, and reduced financial anxiety during economic uncertainty.

In today's economy, many households face rising living costs, inflation pressure, higher insurance premiums, increasing taxes, and economic unpredictability. Because of this, financial resilience has become more important than ever. Reducing mortgage debt can function as a form of financial defense. A homeowner with a significantly reduced mortgage balance often has more options during recessions, business slowdowns, health emergencies, or income interruptions.

Equity becomes a financial shield that provides both security and opportunity. This book will also explore how different types of income can be redirected toward mortgage acceleration. Many people underestimate the power of side income because they focus only on their primary salary. However, modern wealth creation increasingly comes from multiple income streams. Freelancing, consulting, online businesses, digital products, rental income, commission work, content creation, affiliate marketing, coaching, investing, and entrepreneurship all create opportunities for additional cash flow. Even relatively small secondary income streams can become powerful mortgage payoff tools when applied consistently over time.

You will learn how to create structured payoff systems rather than relying on random extra payments. Consistency and planning often outperform emotional decisions. Some homeowners use percentage-based systems where a fixed portion of bonuses or side income automatically goes toward mortgage reduction. Others establish milestone-based payoff targets. Some use quarterly lump sum strategies. Others combine mortgage acceleration with investing or real estate acquisition. There is no single perfect strategy for everyone because every homeowner has different income patterns, risk tolerance, financial goals, and investment opportunities.

The psychological impact of mortgage reduction is another major theme throughout this book. Debt affects behavior in ways many people do not fully recognize. Monthly obligations create pressure, influence decision-making, and shape emotional well-being. As debt decreases, confidence often rises. Financial independence becomes more realistic. Stress levels frequently decline. Many homeowners report feeling emotionally lighter as principal balances shrink because they begin to see a future where mandatory monthly obligations no longer dominate their lives.

This book will also discuss common mistakes people make when using lump sums. Some homeowners apply too much cash toward principal while neglecting emergency reserves. Others aggressively pay down low-interest debt while ignoring high-interest liabilities such as credit cards or personal loans. Some fail to analyze investment alternatives that could potentially outperform mortgage payoff. Others refinance incorrectly or fail to understand prepayment rules and lender servicing procedures. True financial intelligence comes from understanding both the advantages and limitations of aggressive payoff strategies.

Another important lesson throughout this series is that mortgage freedom is not simply about eliminating debt—it is about creating options. A paid-off home changes the financial structure of a household. Cash flow improves significantly. Risk exposure declines. Investment flexibility expands. Families often gain the ability to save more aggressively, invest more consistently, help children financially, travel more freely, or reduce work obligations. Mortgage elimination becomes a tool for designing life on your own terms rather than remaining trapped inside decades of mandatory payments.

The strategies discussed in this book are designed for a wide range of individuals, including salaried employees, business owners, self-employed professionals, commission earners, investors, retirees, and families working toward long-term financial independence. Whether your goal is complete mortgage elimination within ten years, reducing interest expense substantially, improving monthly cash flow, or building long-term wealth more efficiently, the principles inside this book can help you develop a structured plan aligned with your personal goals.

As you continue through this book, you will learn how to analyze your current mortgage, identify payoff opportunities, calculate interest savings, prioritize lump sum timing, and create a long-term payoff roadmap that balances debt reduction with wealth creation. You will also learn how disciplined financial behavior can create momentum that compounds over time. Small strategic actions repeated consistently often produce life-changing financial outcomes. Mortgage freedom is rarely achieved accidentally. It is usually the result of intentional planning, disciplined execution, and intelligent financial choices made consistently over many years. Every extra dollar directed strategically toward principal has the potential to reduce future financial pressure and accelerate independence. The process may begin with a single bonus payment, a side hustle check, or a tax refund, but over time those decisions can completely reshape a person's financial future.

The purpose of this book is not merely to help you pay off a mortgage faster. The deeper purpose is to help you think differently about money, cash flow, debt, opportunity, and long-term wealth. Once you understand how to redirect temporary income increases into permanent financial advantages, you begin operating differently from the average consumer. You stop thinking only about spending and start thinking strategically about ownership, leverage, equity, freedom, and financial control.

The journey toward mortgage freedom often begins with one decision: choosing to use money intentionally instead of automatically. That decision alone can change the course of your financial future forever.

Chapter 1

Understanding the True Power of Lump Sum Mortgage Payments

Most homeowners spend years believing that paying off a mortgage early requires extraordinary income, extreme budgeting, or unrealistic sacrifices. Many assume that mortgage freedom is reserved only for the wealthy or financially gifted. However, one of the biggest financial secrets in real estate and personal finance is that even ordinary people with average incomes can dramatically reduce their mortgage balance and eliminate years of payments through strategic lump sum contributions. Understanding how these payments work is the foundation for unlocking faster financial freedom, stronger cash flow, and long-term wealth acceleration.

A lump sum mortgage payment is any large payment applied directly toward the principal balance of a mortgage outside the normal required monthly payment schedule. Unlike standard monthly payments, which are divided between interest and principal according to the lender's amortization schedule, lump sum payments directly attack the remaining loan balance. This distinction is extremely important because the remaining principal balance determines how much future interest the lender can charge over time. The smaller the balance becomes, the less interest accumulates moving forward.

Most homeowners never fully study how mortgage amortization functions. They simply make their monthly payment and assume progress is occurring naturally. While the balance does decrease gradually over time, the reality is that during the early years of a mortgage, the majority of each payment goes toward interest rather than principal. This means borrowers are often paying thousands of dollars every year while only reducing the actual loan balance by a relatively small amount. Understanding this system changes the way financially educated homeowners approach debt repayment.

For example, a homeowner with a 30-year mortgage may spend the first five to seven years paying mostly interest. During this period, the lender earns a significant amount of profit while the borrower builds equity slowly. Many borrowers become frustrated when they realize that after years of payments, their mortgage balance has barely moved. This is why lump sum payments can become such a powerful financial weapon. Instead of waiting for gradual amortization to slowly reduce the balance, the borrower interrupts the interest cycle directly by making substantial principal reductions.

One of the most important concepts in mortgage acceleration is timing. A lump sum payment made early in a loan often creates significantly greater savings than the same payment made later. This occurs because early principal reductions eliminate future interest before it has time to accumulate over decades. The earlier a borrower reduces principal, the longer the lender loses the ability to charge interest on that portion of the debt.

Consider a homeowner who applies a $20,000 lump sum payment during the third year of a mortgage. That payment not only reduces the balance immediately, but it also prevents future interest from accumulating on that $20,000 over the remaining decades of the loan. In many cases, the actual long-term savings can be substantially higher than the original lump sum itself. This is one of the reasons financially disciplined individuals often prioritize principal reduction whenever they experience increased income opportunities.

Many people underestimate how often lump sum opportunities appear throughout life. These opportunities are not limited to inheritances or lottery winnings. In reality, many households experience multiple periods of excess cash flow that could potentially accelerate mortgage freedom if used strategically. Examples include work bonuses, tax refunds, commission income, overtime pay, side hustle profits, business revenue spikes, stock gains, property sales, gifts, insurance settlements, legal settlements, or even reduced monthly expenses during certain periods.

Unfortunately, most individuals never develop a structured system for handling financial windfalls. Instead of using these opportunities strategically, many people increase lifestyle spending immediately after receiving extra money. A large tax refund becomes a shopping trip. A work bonus becomes a luxury purchase. A profitable business month becomes an excuse for unnecessary expenses. Over time, these habits prevent long-term wealth accumulation because temporary income increases disappear quickly without improving the individual's permanent financial position.

Financially intelligent homeowners behave differently. They understand that every lump sum payment represents an opportunity to buy back future freedom. Instead of viewing extra income only as spending money, they view it as leverage. They understand that reducing debt permanently lowers future obligations and increases future flexibility. This mindset shift often separates financially stable households from those trapped in long-term financial stress despite earning high incomes.

Another critical advantage of lump sum mortgage reduction is the emotional and psychological benefit it creates. Debt carries emotional weight whether people openly acknowledge it or not. Mortgage obligations influence career decisions, business risks, retirement timelines, lifestyle choices, and overall stress levels. Many individuals feel pressure knowing they owe hundreds of thousands of dollars on their home. As the balance decreases faster, many borrowers experience increased confidence, reduced anxiety, and greater long-term clarity.

The psychological momentum of mortgage reduction can also create improved financial discipline in other areas of life. Once homeowners begin seeing significant progress, they often become more motivated to save, invest, and manage money strategically. Momentum matters greatly in personal finance. Small victories create confidence, and confidence creates consistency. Over time, consistent financial decisions compound into major life-changing results.

However, effective lump sum strategies require balance. One of the biggest mistakes homeowners make is becoming overly aggressive without maintaining proper liquidity. Some individuals use nearly all available cash to reduce mortgage debt while leaving themselves financially vulnerable. This can create problems during emergencies, job losses, medical events, or unexpected expenses. Mortgage payoff should strengthen financial stability, not weaken it. Maintaining emergency reserves and proper cash flow remains essential.

Another common mistake involves ignoring high-interest debt while focusing only on mortgage reduction. In many situations, it makes more financial sense to eliminate credit card debt, personal loans, or other high-interest liabilities before aggressively attacking a lower-interest mortgage. Financial strategy requires prioritization. Mortgage payoff can be powerful, but it should be part of a broader financial plan rather than an emotional reaction.

Interest rate environment also matters. A homeowner with a very low fixed mortgage rate may decide to balance mortgage acceleration with investing, business expansion, or real estate acquisitions that potentially generate higher returns. On the other hand, a homeowner carrying a higher mortgage interest rate may prioritize payoff more aggressively. There is no universal formula that applies equally to everyone because every financial situation contains different goals, risks, income structures, and opportunities.

One of the greatest benefits of mortgage reduction is the improvement in future monthly cash flow. Once the mortgage disappears, a significant monthly obligation vanishes permanently. This can dramatically change retirement planning, investment capability, career flexibility, and overall lifestyle freedom. Many homeowners discover that once the mortgage is eliminated, they can redirect those former mortgage payments toward investing, business ownership, travel, charitable giving, family support, or early retirement goals.

This chapter is not designed to convince you to blindly throw every dollar into your mortgage. Instead, the purpose is to help you understand the true power of strategic principal reduction and how lump sum payments can accelerate wealth creation when used intelligently. Mortgage payoff is not simply about eliminating debt. It is about increasing ownership, reducing risk, improving cash flow, and creating greater control over your future.

As you move through this book, you will learn how to identify the best opportunities for lump sum payments, how to calculate potential interest savings, how to avoid common mistakes, and how to structure a payoff system aligned with your personal financial goals. Some readers may pursue aggressive mortgage elimination within ten years. Others may focus on partial acceleration while continuing to invest heavily. Both approaches can succeed when implemented strategically.

The key lesson is this: every lump sum payment creates a permanent improvement in your financial position. Unlike temporary purchases that lose value over time, principal reduction permanently lowers debt and future interest obligations. The effects continue compounding for years. Even modest extra payments, when repeated consistently, can dramatically shorten a mortgage and improve long-term wealth.

The mortgage lender profits most when borrowers follow the exact minimum payment schedule for thirty years. Financially educated homeowners understand they are not required to remain on that path. Through intentional strategy, discipline, and intelligent use of financial opportunities, borrowers can rewrite the timeline completely. They can reduce decades of debt into years, reclaim interest that would otherwise be lost, and create financial freedom much faster than most people believe possible.

The journey toward mortgage acceleration begins with awareness. Once homeowners understand how the system works, they stop viewing lump sums as random financial events and begin seeing them as powerful tools for wealth creation. That perspective alone can transform a family's long-term financial future.

The Bonus Check That Changed Everything

Michael Ramirez had spent most of his adult life believing that mortgages were simply a permanent part of adulthood. At forty-two years old, he lived in a comfortable suburban home with his wife Elena and their two children. He worked as a regional sales manager for a construction supply company in Florida, earning a stable income that supported the family well enough to stay current on bills, take occasional vacations, and maintain a respectable middle-class lifestyle. On paper, everything looked successful. Yet every month when the mortgage payment left his bank account, Michael felt the same frustration deep inside.

He still owed more than $420,000 on a mortgage that felt endless. Even after years of payments, the balance barely seemed to move. He often joked with friends that the bank owned more of his home than he did. Although he laughed outwardly, the reality bothered him deeply. He disliked the feeling of obligation hanging over his family year after year. He dreamed about a future where the mortgage no longer controlled his monthly decisions.

One Friday afternoon near the end of the year, Michael received unexpected news during a company meeting. His division had exceeded sales projections by a large margin, and upper management announced substantial performance bonuses for senior employees. Michael stared quietly at the email confirmation later that afternoon. His bonus would total nearly $38,000 before taxes.

At first, excitement took over immediately. His mind raced with possibilities. He imagined upgrading his SUV, taking the family to Europe, remodeling the kitchen, and finally buying the luxury watch he had admired online for years. After all, he worked hard. He deserved to enjoy the money.

That evening, he showed Elena the bonus letter while they sat at the kitchen table after dinner. She smiled proudly and hugged him tightly. For a few minutes they talked excitedly about vacations, shopping, and celebrating. But later that night, after the children went to sleep, Elena asked a simple question that changed everything.

"What if we used part of it to get ahead financially instead of just spending it?"

Michael leaned back in his chair quietly. "What do you mean?"

"I mean the mortgage," she replied softly. "We always talk about how stressful it feels. What if this is an opportunity to finally make real progress?"

Michael initially resisted the idea. The thought of putting such a large amount toward the mortgage felt almost painful.

Spending money brought immediate excitement. Mortgage reduction felt invisible and boring. Yet over the next few days, Elena continued discussing the idea calmly. She showed him mortgage payoff calculators online. She explained how principal reductions worked. Together they reviewed their amortization schedule for the first time in years.

Michael was shocked.

He discovered that despite years of payments, the majority of his earlier payments had gone toward interest. Even more shocking was the realization that a large principal payment early in the loan could potentially save enormous amounts in future interest.

For the first time, the mortgage no longer felt like a fixed prison sentence. It suddenly appeared flexible. Controllable. Beat-able.

Instead of spending the entire bonus, Michael and Elena decided on a balanced strategy. They allocated part of the money for family enjoyment, paid off a small credit card balance, strengthened their emergency savings, and directed $25,000 directly toward the mortgage principal.

The following month, Michael logged into the mortgage portal and saw the updated balance. Something changed emotionally in that moment. For the first time in years, he felt momentum. Real progress. He realized that a single decision had permanently reduced years of future interest and brought his family measurably closer to freedom.

That feeling became addictive. Over the next year, Michael approached money differently. Instead of automatically increasing lifestyle spending every time extra income appeared, he began analyzing opportunities strategically. He started a small consulting side business helping local contractors improve their sales systems. Initially, the side income was inconsistent, bringing in only a few hundred dollars monthly. But Michael applied nearly every dollar directly toward the mortgage.

Slowly, the balance began dropping faster than ever before.

Each reduction motivated him further. He became more intentional with spending. He negotiated insurance rates, reduced unnecessary subscriptions, and redirected wasteful expenses toward principal. None of the changes felt extreme. He still enjoyed life. He still traveled occasionally and spent time with family. The difference was that he now viewed every dollar through the lens of long-term freedom instead of temporary excitement.

Two years later, Michael received another major bonus at work. This time the decision felt easier. Instead of emotional spending, he immediately developed a strategic allocation plan. A portion went to investing, a portion strengthened liquidity, and another significant amount reduced the mortgage principal again. By age forty-seven, Michael and Elena had reduced their mortgage balance by more than half compared to the original amortization schedule. Friends and relatives began asking how they were progressing so quickly. Many assumed Michael had received a massive inheritance or secret financial advantage. In reality, the transformation came from repeated intentional decisions.

What surprised Michael most was how the mortgage payoff journey changed his mindset beyond finances. He felt calmer. More confident. Less trapped by work stress. Because the mortgage balance had dropped so aggressively, he no longer felt terrified of career uncertainty. He began considering investment opportunities and business ventures that once seemed too risky.

The reduction in debt created psychological freedom long before the mortgage was fully eliminated.

One evening, Michael sat alone on his backyard patio reviewing their latest mortgage statement. The remaining balance had fallen below six figures for the first time. He stared at the number quietly while thinking about how different life felt compared to five years earlier.

Back then, he believed mortgages controlled people forever.

Now he understood something completely different. Mortgages could be controlled strategically by disciplined homeowners willing to think long term.

The bonus check that once seemed like temporary spending money had become the beginning of a completely different financial future. Not because of luck. Not because of perfection. But because one intentional decision created momentum that compounded over time.

And for the first time in his adult life, Michael could clearly see the finish line ahead.

Chapter 2

The Mathematics of Mortgage Interest and Why Early Lump Sum Payments Matter Most

One of the greatest financial advantages a homeowner can gain is understanding how mortgage interest truly works. Most borrowers focus only on the monthly payment because that is the number they see every month leaving their bank account. However, financially intelligent homeowners understand that the monthly payment tells only a small part of the story. The real financial battle exists inside the structure of amortization, where lenders collect the majority of their profits during the early years of a mortgage. Once borrowers fully understand this system, they begin to see why early lump sum payments can dramatically reduce years of debt and save enormous amounts of money.

A mortgage is not a simple equal-payment arrangement where every payment reduces debt evenly over time. Instead, mortgages are designed using amortization schedules that heavily prioritize interest collection during the beginning years of the loan. This means lenders receive most of their profit early while borrowers build equity slowly. The longer the borrower remains on the original payment schedule, the more total interest the lender ultimately collects.

For example, many homeowners are surprised to discover that during the first several years of a 30-year mortgage, a substantial portion of every payment goes toward interest instead of principal reduction. A borrower may make thousands of dollars in monthly payments while only reducing the actual loan balance by a few hundred dollars each month. This reality explains why many people feel frustrated after years of payments when they realize their balance has barely decreased.

Understanding amortization changes the way homeowners think about debt. Instead of blindly following the lender's schedule, strategic borrowers begin looking for opportunities to reduce principal aggressively during the periods when interest costs are highest. This is why timing matters so much in mortgage acceleration. The earlier a lump sum payment is made, the greater the long-term impact often becomes.

The larger the remaining principal balance, the more interest the lender earns every month. Therefore, when borrowers reduce principal early through lump sum payments, they weaken the lender's future ability to collect interest. To fully understand this concept, imagine two homeowners with identical mortgages. Both borrowers have a $500,000 mortgage at a fixed interest rate over thirty years. The first homeowner simply makes minimum payments according to the original schedule. The second homeowner applies a $25,000 lump sum payment during the second year of the mortgage.

At first glance, the difference may not appear dramatic. After all, both borrowers still owe substantial balances. However, the long-term effects become enormous because the second borrower permanently eliminated future interest accumulation on that $25,000. Over decades, this single action may save tens of thousands of dollars while also shortening the mortgage payoff timeline significantly.

This is the hidden power of early principal reduction. Mortgage interest compounds against borrowers over time, but strategic principal reduction reverses the process. Every dollar removed from the balance early weakens future interest accumulation permanently. The effects continue compounding month after month for the remaining life of the loan.

Another important reality is that most homeowners underestimate how much total interest they will pay over thirty years. Many borrowers focus only on whether they can afford the monthly payment rather than calculating the true long-term cost of financing. In reality, homeowners often pay hundreds of thousands of dollars in interest over the life of a large mortgage. The bank may ultimately receive an amount approaching or even exceeding the original purchase price of the property itself depending on interest rates and loan terms.

This is why mortgage acceleration can become such a powerful wealth-building strategy. Every dollar saved in future interest becomes money retained by the homeowner instead of transferred to the lender. Over time, these savings can be redirected toward investing, business ownership, retirement planning, education funding, or additional real estate acquisitions.

One of the biggest psychological shifts occurs when homeowners stop viewing lump sum payments as "losing cash" and begin viewing them as "buying future freedom." A principal reduction is not merely a payment—it is a permanent reduction in future obligations. Every aggressive payment creates future monthly flexibility and lowers long-term financial pressure.

The earlier these reductions occur, the greater the impact tends to become. A $10,000 payment during year two may create dramatically larger savings than the same payment during year twenty-five because the early payment prevents decades of future interest from accumulating. Time amplifies the effectiveness of principal reduction. This concept is very similar to long-term investing. Just as investments compound positively over time, mortgage interest compounds negatively against borrowers over time. Homeowners who understand this relationship begin treating lump sum payments as a form of guaranteed financial return. Reducing debt lowers risk while simultaneously increasing future cash flow.

Another major advantage of early mortgage reduction is equity growth. Equity represents ownership in the property rather than ownership held by the lender. The faster the balance decreases, the faster the homeowner builds true financial ownership. Increased equity improves financial stability and can create additional opportunities in the future.

For example, homeowners with substantial equity often have more flexibility during economic downturns. They may qualify for better refinancing terms, home equity financing, investment opportunities, or lower financial stress during emergencies. Equity can become a financial shield protecting the household from uncertainty.

Many financially successful individuals intentionally combine lump sum mortgage strategies with periods of increased income. Instead of allowing every raise or bonus to permanently inflate lifestyle expenses, they allocate portions toward principal reduction. This creates a compounding cycle where increased income accelerates wealth instead of simply increasing consumption.

Lifestyle inflation is one of the greatest financial traps facing modern households. As income rises, spending often rises equally or even faster. Larger homes, luxury vehicles, expensive vacations, subscriptions, dining habits, and unnecessary purchases consume the benefits of higher earnings. Despite making more money, many households remain financially stressed because obligations expand alongside income.

Strategic homeowners interrupt this cycle. Instead of spending every increase in income, they redirect portions toward permanent financial improvements. Mortgage reduction becomes one of the most powerful tools because it creates guaranteed long-term benefits that continue indefinitely.

This does not mean homeowners should eliminate all enjoyment from life. Financial balance remains important. Some lump sums may be divided between investing, lifestyle goals, emergency savings, and mortgage reduction. The key lesson is intentionality. Wealthy financial behavior is often less about income level and more about disciplined decision-making.

Another important factor to understand is interest rate comparison. In certain situations, homeowners may choose to invest excess funds instead of aggressively paying down a low-interest mortgage. If investment opportunities produce substantially higher returns than the mortgage interest rate, balanced strategies may create greater long-term wealth. However, this decision depends heavily on personal risk tolerance, market conditions, financial stability, and investment knowledge.

Mortgage payoff should never become purely emotional or ideological. Some individuals aggressively eliminate low-interest debt while neglecting investment opportunities that could produce superior long-term returns. Others become so focused on investing that they ignore the emotional and financial security benefits of reduced debt. Intelligent financial planning requires evaluating both mathematics and personal lifestyle goals.

One major emotional benefit of mortgage reduction is decreased financial vulnerability. Large debt obligations create pressure during uncertain times. Economic recessions, job losses, health issues, or business slowdowns become more stressful when major monthly obligations remain high. Reduced debt improves resilience and creates breathing room during difficult periods. Many homeowners underestimate how much confidence comes from lower debt levels. As mortgage balances shrink, financial fear often decreases. Individuals feel more capable of taking career risks, launching businesses, investing strategically, or pursuing opportunities they once avoided. Debt reduction creates flexibility that extends beyond simple mathematics.

Another overlooked benefit involves retirement planning. Homeowners who eliminate mortgages before retirement dramatically reduce their required monthly expenses later in life. This lowers the amount of retirement savings needed to maintain financial stability. A paid-off home often becomes one of the strongest foundations for long-term retirement security.

This chapter is designed to help you understand that mortgage payoff is not merely about making extra payments randomly. It is about understanding the mathematics behind debt and using that knowledge strategically. Once borrowers understand how interest accumulates, they begin making financial decisions differently.

Every principal reduction weakens future interest accumulation. Every early payment creates larger long-term savings potential. Every intentional financial decision builds momentum toward increased freedom and reduced obligation.

The lender's business model depends on borrowers remaining in debt for decades. Financially educated homeowners recognize they have the ability to alter that timeline significantly through strategy and discipline. The sooner this understanding develops, the greater the opportunity for long-term financial transformation.

Mortgage freedom is not simply about eliminating a payment. It is about reclaiming years of future cash flow, reducing financial stress, increasing ownership, and creating greater control over your life. Once homeowners truly understand the mathematics of interest, they stop viewing mortgages as fixed lifelong obligations and begin seeing them as financial systems that can be strategically accelerated.

The Engineer Who Finally Understood the Numbers

David Mercer had always considered himself intelligent with money. As a mechanical engineer in Orlando, he earned a six-figure salary, contributed consistently to retirement accounts, maintained excellent credit, and avoided reckless spending. Friends often asked him for financial advice because he appeared organized and successful from the outside. Yet despite all his planning, one thing quietly bothered him for years.

His mortgage balance barely seemed to move.

At forty-five years old, David had owned his home for nearly eight years. Every month he made the mortgage payment automatically without fail. The process had become routine. He rarely thought deeply about the loan because he assumed mortgages simply worked slowly over time. After all, thirty years was normal. Everyone around him carried mortgage debt.

One evening, while reviewing financial statements for tax preparation, David noticed something unsettling. Despite paying nearly $200,000 toward the mortgage over the years, the principal balance had decreased far less than he expected. Curious and slightly irritated, he pulled up his amortization schedule online for the first time in years.

As he scrolled through the numbers, confusion turned into frustration.

He realized the majority of his early payments had gone toward interest instead of principal. Month after month, year after year, the lender had collected enormous amounts of interest while the actual debt reduction remained relatively small.

David stared silently at the screen.

"How is this possible?" he muttered.

His wife Lauren walked into the office carrying tea and noticed the expression on his face.

"What happened?" she asked. David pointed at the screen. "We've been paying this thing for almost eight years, and it feels like we barely own any more of the house than before."

Lauren sat beside him quietly while he explained the numbers. Together they reviewed the amortization schedule line by line. For the first time, both of them truly understood how heavily front-loaded mortgage interest was during the early years.

The realization changed something inside David immediately.

As an engineer, he loved systems and optimization. Once he understood how the mortgage mathematically functioned, he stopped viewing it emotionally and began viewing it strategically. He realized the lender's entire profit model depended on borrowers staying on schedule for decades.

And suddenly he wanted out.

Over the next several weeks, David became obsessed with mortgage payoff calculations. He built spreadsheets comparing different payoff scenarios. He tested how various lump sum payments altered the timeline. The results shocked him repeatedly.

A single large principal reduction early in the loan created enormous long-term savings.

For years, David and Lauren had received annual bonuses from work and spent most of them upgrading lifestyle expenses. Some years they renovated parts of the house. Other years they upgraded vehicles or traveled internationally. While they enjoyed those experiences, they suddenly realized none of those purchases permanently improved their financial position.

David approached Lauren one Saturday morning while holding printed spreadsheets.

"If we redirect our next bonuses toward the mortgage," he explained carefully, "we could potentially remove almost a decade from this loan."

Lauren raised her eyebrows. "Seriously?"

David nodded. "The interest savings are massive because we're still early enough in the loan."

The conversation marked a turning point for the family.

That year, instead of spending their bonuses impulsively, they allocated nearly $40,000 toward the mortgage principal. At first, the payment felt emotionally uncomfortable. Watching such a large amount leave their savings account triggered anxiety. But several weeks later, when the updated mortgage balance appeared online, both David and Lauren felt something unexpected.

Relief.

For the first time, the mortgage no longer felt infinite.

David became increasingly disciplined after that moment. Every raise, bonus, consulting payment, and tax refund became an opportunity for strategic principal reduction. He still invested regularly and maintained emergency reserves, but now every financial decision included one important question:

“Does this improve our long-term freedom?”

The question changed everything.

Over the next three years, David dramatically accelerated the mortgage payoff timeline. The family did not live miserably. They still enjoyed vacations, family activities, and occasional luxuries. The difference was intentionality. They stopped wasting financial opportunities on temporary excitement and started focusing on permanent improvement.

One afternoon during lunch at work, David overheard coworkers discussing rising mortgage rates and financial stress. Several complained about feeling trapped by debt for the next thirty years.

David smiled quietly because he no longer felt trapped himself.

The mathematics had changed his mindset completely. Instead of viewing the mortgage as a lifelong burden, he now viewed it as a solvable equation. Every principal payment weakened the lender's position and strengthened his own future freedom. The process became motivating instead of discouraging.

At age fifty, David reviewed their updated payoff projection. If they continued their current strategy, the mortgage could potentially disappear more than twelve years early.

Lauren looked at the numbers in disbelief.

"That's an entire decade of payments we don't have to make," she whispered.

David nodded slowly.

"And think about what that means," he replied. "That's freedom. That's flexibility. That's years of our lives where our income belongs to us instead of the bank."

For several moments they sat quietly together at the kitchen table.

Then Lauren smiled.

"All because you finally looked at the numbers."

David laughed softly. "No," he replied. "All because we finally understood how the system actually works."

And from that moment forward, every lump sum payment stopped feeling like a sacrifice and started feeling like progress toward a completely different future.

Chapter 3

Using Work Bonuses, Commissions, and Side Income to Accelerate Mortgage Freedom

One of the fastest ways homeowners can dramatically reduce mortgage debt is by strategically redirecting temporary increases in income toward principal reduction. While many people focus only on cutting expenses to pay off debt faster, the truth is that increasing income often creates far more powerful opportunities for financial acceleration. Work bonuses, commissions, side businesses, freelance income, overtime pay, consulting revenue, digital product sales, and entrepreneurial income can become extraordinary tools when used intentionally. The key is not merely earning more money, but learning how to deploy additional income strategically to create permanent financial improvement.

Most households experience fluctuating income throughout life. Even individuals with stable salaries often receive periods of increased earnings through bonuses, raises, incentives, or tax refunds. Sales professionals may earn commissions. Business owners may experience profitable months. Investors may receive distributions or gains. Side hustles may create additional cash flow. Unfortunately, many people automatically absorb increased income into lifestyle inflation instead of using it to strengthen their long-term financial position.

Lifestyle inflation occurs when rising income immediately leads to rising spending. A larger paycheck often triggers larger expenses. A bonus becomes a vacation. A commission becomes luxury shopping. Extra business revenue becomes upgraded cars, dining habits, subscriptions, or unnecessary purchases. Over time, income may rise substantially while financial stress remains unchanged because spending expands equally fast.

This pattern traps many high-income earners financially. From the outside, they appear successful because they earn impressive incomes and own expensive possessions. Yet internally they remain dependent on large monthly cash flow simply to maintain their lifestyle. Debt obligations continue controlling their financial decisions despite years of hard work and increased earnings.

Financially disciplined homeowners approach increased income differently. Instead of allowing every financial gain to disappear into temporary consumption, they intentionally allocate portions toward long-term wealth creation. Mortgage principal reduction becomes one of the most effective strategies because it permanently lowers future obligations while simultaneously increasing equity and financial flexibility.

One of the most important psychological shifts occurs when homeowners stop viewing bonuses and side income as "extra spending money" and begin viewing them as "financial acceleration tools." This mindset transformation changes decision-making completely. Instead of asking, "What can I buy?" individuals begin asking, "How can this money permanently improve my future?"

The answer often lies in principal reduction.

Every lump sum payment applied toward a mortgage creates a permanent financial improvement. Unlike temporary purchases that lose value quickly, principal reduction lowers future interest obligations forever. This means every strategic payment improves future cash flow, shortens the mortgage timeline, and reduces long-term financial pressure.

Many homeowners underestimate the long-term impact of relatively small side income streams. A freelance project earning several hundred dollars monthly may not appear life-changing initially. However, when consistently directed toward mortgage principal, the results can become extraordinary over time. A side hustle generating an additional $1,000 per month could potentially remove years from a mortgage while saving substantial interest. The modern economy offers more opportunities for side income than ever before in history. Technology and digital platforms have created countless ways for individuals to monetize skills, knowledge, creativity, or services outside traditional employment. Consulting, coaching, online courses, affiliate marketing, freelance work, content creation, digital publishing, rental income, ecommerce, social media monetization, AI-powered services, and real estate investing all create opportunities for additional cash flow.

The true power of side income is not merely the income itself—it is the ability to redirect money that is not required for basic survival. When homeowners apply side income directly toward mortgage reduction, they often accelerate payoff without significantly affecting their primary lifestyle. This creates a psychological advantage because progress occurs without feeling heavily deprived.

For example, a homeowner may choose to dedicate 100% of annual bonuses toward principal reduction while continuing to live primarily on base salary income. Another homeowner may direct all commission income above a certain threshold toward the mortgage. Others may commit all side hustle income to debt elimination for a fixed number of years. Structured systems like these create consistency and remove emotional decision-making. Automation can also strengthen mortgage acceleration strategies. Some individuals automatically transfer a fixed percentage of every bonus or commission directly toward principal immediately after receiving it. By removing the temptation to spend first and save later, automation creates disciplined financial momentum.

Another important concept involves separating temporary income from permanent income. Many people make dangerous financial mistakes by increasing recurring monthly obligations based on inconsistent income streams. For example, individuals may buy expensive cars or luxury homes assuming bonuses or commissions will continue forever. When income fluctuates unexpectedly, financial pressure increases dramatically.

Strategic homeowners often avoid this trap by using variable income for one-time principal reductions rather than permanent lifestyle expansion. This creates greater long-term stability because debt decreases instead of obligations increasing.

High-income earners especially benefit from understanding this principle. Many professionals earning six-figure or seven-figure incomes remain financially stressed because spending rises proportionally with earnings. Mortgage debt, luxury expenses, and lifestyle obligations consume income continuously. In contrast, disciplined individuals who redirect portions of high income toward principal reduction often create financial independence much faster despite earning similar salaries.

Another overlooked benefit of mortgage reduction through increased income is the emotional confidence it creates. Many individuals feel trapped by dependence on their primary job because their fixed monthly obligations remain extremely high. As debt decreases, flexibility increases. Homeowners often feel more capable of pursuing entrepreneurship, career changes, investments, or lifestyle improvements because financial pressure gradually declines.

The relationship between income and debt also affects stress levels significantly. Individuals carrying large mortgage obligations frequently experience anxiety during economic downturns, layoffs, or business slowdowns. Accelerated payoff reduces vulnerability and increases resilience during uncertain periods.

Tax refunds represent another commonly overlooked opportunity for mortgage acceleration. Many households receive thousands of dollars annually through refunds yet spend the money impulsively because it feels separate from normal income. Financially disciplined homeowners often treat refunds strategically by allocating portions toward principal reduction, emergency savings, or investments.

The same principle applies to inheritance money, profit-sharing distributions, stock compensation, and unexpected financial gains. Every financial windfall presents a choice between temporary consumption and permanent improvement. While balanced enjoyment remains important, homeowners who consistently prioritize strategic principal reduction often transform their long-term financial future dramatically.

However, balance remains essential. Mortgage acceleration should not eliminate all investing, emergency savings, or quality of life. Some individuals become overly obsessed with debt elimination while neglecting diversification, liquidity, or long-term investment opportunities. Intelligent financial planning requires evaluating multiple factors including interest rates, retirement goals, tax strategy, risk tolerance, and future opportunities.

For example, a homeowner with a very low fixed mortgage interest rate and strong investment opportunities may choose a balanced approach between investing and principal reduction. Another homeowner with higher interest debt or unstable income may prioritize aggressive payoff more heavily. Personal finance remains deeply personal.

The key lesson is intentionality.

Most financial success comes not from random luck but from repeated strategic decisions made consistently over time. A homeowner who repeatedly redirects bonuses, side income, commissions, and financial windfalls toward principal reduction often creates extraordinary long-term results without needing extreme sacrifice.

Small consistent actions compound powerfully. A single bonus payment may not eliminate a mortgage immediately, but repeated strategic payments over years can shorten the timeline dramatically. Momentum builds slowly at first and then accelerates increasingly over time.

Another important advantage of increased income directed toward mortgage payoff is behavioral reinforcement. Every visible reduction in the mortgage balance creates motivation. Homeowners begin seeing measurable progress instead of feeling trapped inside an endless thirty-year cycle. Confidence grows. Financial habits improve. Discipline strengthens.

The process often spills into other areas of life as well. Individuals who become intentional with debt reduction frequently improve investing habits, savings discipline, spending awareness, and long-term planning overall. Mortgage acceleration becomes part of a broader transformation in financial behavior. As homeowners progress through the mortgage payoff journey, they often discover something unexpected: the goal is not merely eliminating debt. The deeper goal is increasing control over life itself. Reduced debt creates options. It creates flexibility. It creates breathing room. It creates independence from constant financial pressure.

Every bonus redirected strategically toward principal buys back future freedom. Every side hustle payment applied intentionally weakens future obligations. Every commission payment used wisely creates greater ownership instead of greater dependence.

Mortgage freedom rarely occurs accidentally. It is usually built through repeated intentional choices over time. Increased income alone does not create wealth automatically. Strategic deployment of income creates wealth.

Homeowners who understand this principle stop viewing bonuses and side income as opportunities for short-term excitement alone. Instead, they begin seeing every financial gain as an opportunity to permanently strengthen their future. That mindset shift alone can completely change the trajectory of a person's financial life.

The Realtor Who Refused to Stay Broke Despite High Income

Samantha Ellis was one of the top real estate agents in her market. By age thirty-eight, she had built a strong reputation in Orlando for luxury home sales, investment property transactions, and relocation clients. Her social media looked impressive. She drove a luxury SUV, wore designer clothing, and regularly posted photos from upscale restaurants and networking events. From the outside, most people assumed Samantha was wealthy.

The truth was very different.

Despite earning well over $250,000 during some years, Samantha constantly felt financial pressure. Her income fluctuated heavily because commissions were inconsistent. Some months she earned extraordinary amounts. Other months felt painfully slow. Whenever she closed multiple deals, she rewarded herself immediately with shopping, travel, expensive dining, or luxury upgrades because she believed she deserved it after working so hard.

Unfortunately, her spending rose as quickly as her income.

She purchased a large home several years earlier during a strong market year, assuming her commissions would continue growing forever. Although she could technically afford the mortgage during strong months, the large payment created constant stress during slower periods. Every market slowdown triggered anxiety. Every delayed closing affected her emotionally. She felt trapped inside a lifestyle that required continuous high performance simply to maintain stability.

One evening after a particularly stressful month, Samantha sat at her kitchen island reviewing bills and upcoming expenses. Her mortgage payment alone felt enormous. Although she had recently closed several luxury deals, most of the money had already disappeared through spending, taxes, business expenses, and lifestyle costs.

Her friend Natalie stopped by later that evening. Natalie had been Samantha's close friend since college and worked as a financial planner. After listening quietly to Samantha vent about financial stress, Natalie asked a direct question.

"How much of your commission income actually improves your long-term financial position?"

Samantha looked confused.

"What do you mean?"

Natalie leaned forward carefully. "You make great money, Sam. But every time you earn more, you spend more. You're successful, but you still feel financially trapped."

The words stung because Samantha knew they were true.

Natalie continued. "You're treating commission income like permanent lifestyle income instead of strategic opportunity income."

That sentence stayed in Samantha's mind for days.

A week later, she reviewed her previous three years of commissions and spending patterns. The numbers shocked her. She had earned extraordinary income during strong market periods, yet very little remained. Most of the money had flowed toward temporary lifestyle expenses rather than permanent financial improvement.

Then she analyzed her mortgage amortization schedule.

For the first time, Samantha truly understood how much interest the lender would collect over the life of the loan if she followed the standard payment schedule. The total amount made her physically uncomfortable.

Something changed inside her immediately.

Instead of feeling motivated to earn more simply to spend more, she became motivated to buy back her future freedom.

Samantha created a completely new financial system. From that point forward, she committed to directing 40% of every commission check directly toward mortgage principal reduction. Another percentage would cover taxes and investments. Only the remaining portion would support lifestyle spending.

The first month felt emotionally difficult.

After closing a major transaction, Samantha instinctively wanted to celebrate with shopping and luxury purchases. Instead, she wired nearly $18,000 directly toward her mortgage principal.

At first the payment felt painful.

Then she saw the updated mortgage balance.

For the first time in years, she felt real progress.

The feeling surprised her. The principal reduction created more satisfaction than any designer purchase ever had. She realized she had spent years chasing temporary excitement while ignoring the deeper desire underneath everything: freedom.

Over the next two years, Samantha maintained the system relentlessly. Every commission triggered automatic allocations before lifestyle spending occurred. She also launched a small online training program teaching new real estate agents how to generate luxury listings. The additional side income flowed entirely toward mortgage reduction.

As the mortgage balance dropped aggressively, Samantha noticed unexpected emotional changes. Her anxiety during slower sales months declined significantly. Because her debt was shrinking rapidly, she no longer felt desperate for every transaction. She became calmer with clients, more patient in negotiations, and more confident overall.

Ironically, her business performance improved even further.

By age forty-one, Samantha had reduced her mortgage balance by hundreds of thousands of dollars compared to the original schedule. Friends in the real estate industry began asking how she stayed so financially calm during market fluctuations while others constantly panicked.

Most assumed she had inherited money or sold a business.

Very few understood the truth.

The transformation came from changing the direction of her commissions rather than changing the amount she earned.

One evening, Samantha sat alone on her back patio after making another large principal payment from a luxury property closing. The sunset reflected across the pool while she reviewed her updated payoff timeline.

If she continued at the current pace, she could potentially eliminate the mortgage more than fifteen years early.

She leaned back quietly and smiled.

For years, she believed wealth came from looking successful.

Now she understood something much deeper.

Real wealth came from reducing dependence.

Every commission payment redirected toward principal had weakened the financial pressure controlling her life. Every side income payment applied strategically had increased future freedom. The mortgage no longer felt like a lifelong burden. It felt like a shrinking obstacle she was actively defeating.

And for the first time since becoming successful, Samantha no longer felt trapped by the very lifestyle she had worked so hard to build.

Chapter 4

Creating a Strategic Lump Sum Mortgage Payoff Plan That Actually Works

Many homeowners make the mistake of approaching mortgage payoff emotionally rather than strategically. They become excited after hearing stories about people paying off homes early, saving massive amounts of interest, or achieving financial freedom years ahead of schedule. Motivated by emotion, they begin making random extra payments whenever possible without building a structured long-term plan. Although any additional principal payment can help reduce debt, long-term success usually comes from consistency, discipline, and intelligent planning rather than occasional bursts of motivation.

A strategic lump sum mortgage payoff plan is not simply about throwing random amounts of money toward debt whenever extra cash appears. Instead, it is about building a repeatable financial system that aligns with your income patterns, lifestyle goals, emergency needs, investment priorities, and long-term vision for financial freedom. The goal is to create a plan that is sustainable, realistic, and powerful enough to generate momentum over many years.

One of the first steps in building a successful payoff strategy is understanding your current mortgage in detail. Most homeowners know only their monthly payment amount and perhaps the interest rate, but very few fully understand the structure of their loan. Before creating a payoff plan, homeowners should review their remaining balance, interest rate, amortization schedule, loan term, prepayment rules, and projected total interest cost if they continue making only minimum payments.

This process often creates a major psychological wake-up call. Many borrowers become shocked when they calculate how much interest they will ultimately pay over thirty years. In some cases, homeowners may pay amounts approaching or exceeding the original home purchase price in interest alone depending on rates and loan terms. Understanding these numbers changes the way people think about debt. The mortgage stops feeling like a harmless monthly bill and begins looking like a major long-term financial obligation that deserves strategic attention.

Once homeowners understand the true cost of their mortgage, the next step is identifying available lump sum opportunities. Every household has different income patterns and financial strengths. Some individuals receive annual work bonuses. Others earn commissions, overtime pay, profit-sharing distributions, or seasonal business income. Some households generate side hustle revenue, rental income, investment gains, or tax refunds. Others may eventually receive inheritance money, legal settlements, or proceeds from selling assets.

The key is identifying which sources of temporary or irregular income can realistically be redirected toward principal reduction consistently over time. A successful payoff strategy does not require perfection. It requires intentionality and repetition.

One highly effective approach is percentage allocation planning. Instead of waiting to decide emotionally what to do with extra income after receiving it, homeowners establish rules in advance. For example, an individual may commit to directing 50% of all annual bonuses toward mortgage principal. Another may allocate 100% of side hustle income toward debt reduction for five years. Others may apply every tax refund directly to the mortgage automatically.

Predetermined systems create discipline because they reduce emotional spending decisions. Without a plan, unexpected income often disappears quickly into lifestyle inflation. With a structured system, temporary financial opportunities become long-term wealth-building tools.

Another important element of strategic planning involves maintaining proper liquidity. One of the biggest mistakes homeowners make is aggressively paying down mortgage debt while leaving themselves financially vulnerable. Mortgage acceleration should improve financial security rather than create instability. Before directing large lump sums toward principal reduction, homeowners should maintain emergency reserves sufficient to handle job interruptions, medical expenses, repairs, insurance deductibles, and unexpected life events.

A strong emergency fund protects homeowners from needing to rely on high-interest debt during crises. Many financial professionals recommend maintaining at least several months of living expenses in accessible savings before becoming highly aggressive with mortgage payoff strategies.

Another important consideration involves balancing mortgage reduction with investing. Some homeowners carry relatively low fixed mortgage interest rates while simultaneously having opportunities to invest in businesses, retirement accounts, stocks, real estate, or other assets that may produce higher long-term returns. In these situations, the mathematically optimal decision may involve balancing investing and mortgage acceleration rather than focusing entirely on one or the other. Personal finance is never purely mathematical, however. Emotional comfort, risk tolerance, career stability, age, family responsibilities, and lifestyle goals all matter. Some homeowners value the peace of mind that comes from reduced debt even if certain investments could potentially generate higher returns. Others prioritize aggressive investing while maintaining manageable mortgage obligations. There is no universal answer that applies equally to everyone.

The most successful payoff plans are usually personalized rather than copied blindly from someone else's strategy.

Another critical factor in successful mortgage acceleration is automation. Human behavior is often emotional and inconsistent. Without automation, good intentions can easily disappear during busy months or emotionally tempting periods. Many homeowners strengthen their payoff systems by scheduling automatic additional principal payments monthly or automatically transferring portions of bonuses and side income toward the mortgage immediately after receiving them.

Automation removes decision fatigue and strengthens consistency over time. Small repeated actions often produce extraordinary long-term outcomes because momentum compounds gradually.

Tracking progress also plays a major role in maintaining motivation. Mortgage payoff can feel slow initially, especially during the early years. However, visual progress creates emotional reinforcement. Many homeowners stay motivated by tracking balance reductions, interest savings, or years eliminated from the mortgage schedule. Every visible improvement strengthens discipline and reinforces positive financial behavior.

Some individuals create milestone goals to maintain momentum. For example, they may celebrate every $25,000 reduction in principal or each year removed from the payoff timeline. Others focus on reaching psychological milestones such as lowering the balance below certain numbers. Structured progress tracking transforms mortgage acceleration from a vague financial goal into a measurable process.

Income growth strategies can also dramatically accelerate payoff timelines. While reducing expenses remains helpful, increasing income often produces far larger results. Many homeowners pursue side businesses, consulting work, digital products, freelance services, rental income, or entrepreneurial opportunities specifically to generate additional principal reduction funds.

The modern economy provides more income-generation opportunities than ever before. Technology allows individuals to monetize knowledge, skills, creativity, or services globally. Even modest secondary income streams can produce major long-term mortgage acceleration when directed strategically toward principal reduction consistently.

Another important lesson is avoiding comparison with others. Some homeowners become discouraged when comparing their progress to individuals with higher incomes or larger lump sum opportunities. Mortgage acceleration is deeply personal. Every additional principal payment improves financial positioning regardless of size. A homeowner consistently applying smaller lump sums may still save enormous amounts over time through discipline and consistency.

Patience matters tremendously because mortgage acceleration often compounds slowly at first and then accelerates more dramatically later. Early reductions lower future interest accumulation, creating increasing momentum over time. Homeowners who remain consistent frequently experience payoff acceleration that becomes increasingly motivating as balances shrink.

Another common mistake homeowners make is neglecting quality of life completely while pursuing mortgage freedom aggressively. Financial discipline should improve life rather than create misery. Some individuals become so obsessed with payoff goals that they eliminate all enjoyment, vacations, hobbies, or experiences unnecessarily. Sustainable financial plans usually balance long-term discipline with healthy living.

The objective is not merely eliminating debt as quickly as possible at any emotional cost. The objective is building a life with greater freedom, flexibility, and financial security while still enjoying meaningful experiences along the journey.

Mortgage payoff plans should also evolve over time. Income changes, family situations shift, interest rates fluctuate, investment opportunities appear, and priorities develop differently through various stages of life. A strategy that works perfectly at age thirty-five may require adjustments at age fifty-five. Financial flexibility and periodic review remain important.

One of the most powerful benefits of strategic payoff planning is reduced financial stress. Large debt obligations influence nearly every area of life. They affect career decisions, retirement planning, investment risk tolerance, family choices, and emotional well-being. As mortgage balances decline steadily, many homeowners feel increased confidence, stability, and peace of mind.

Reduced debt also creates future cash flow freedom. Once the mortgage disappears, the former monthly payment can be redirected toward investing, retirement accounts, business opportunities, travel, family support, charitable giving, or lifestyle flexibility. Mortgage elimination is not merely about removing debt—it is about reclaiming control over future income.

A strategic payoff plan transforms mortgage reduction from a vague dream into an achievable process. The difference between homeowners who eventually achieve mortgage freedom early and those who remain trapped for decades often comes down to one thing: intentional consistent action.

Every lump sum payment creates permanent progress. Every strategic financial decision weakens future obligations. Every disciplined action compounds over time.

Mortgage freedom rarely occurs accidentally. It is usually engineered through structure, patience, discipline, and intelligent long-term planning.

How a Strategic Lump Sum Plan Can Save Hundreds of Thousands

Let's examine a realistic example of how a homeowner can dramatically accelerate mortgage payoff using a structured lump sum strategy.

Mortgage Details

- Home Purchase Price: $650,000
- Down Payment: $50,000
- Mortgage Amount: $600,000
- Loan Type: 30-Year Fixed Mortgage
- Interest Rate: 6.5%
- Monthly Principal & Interest Payment: Approximately $3,792
- Total Payments Over 30 Years: Approximately $1,365,120
- Total Interest Paid Over 30 Years: Approximately $765,120

At first glance, many homeowners focus only on the monthly payment of about $3,792. However, the real shock comes from the total interest cost. Over thirty years, the borrower would pay approximately $765,120 in interest alone if only minimum payments are made.

Now let's see what happens when the homeowner creates a strategic lump sum payoff system.

The Homeowner's Strategy

The homeowner commits to the following:

- $10,000 annual work bonus applied toward principal every year
- $5,000 annual tax refund applied toward principal every year
- $1,000 monthly side hustle income applied toward principal

This creates:

- Annual Lump Sum Contributions: $15,000
- Monthly Extra Principal Payments: $1,000

New Effective Monthly Payment

Original Payment:

- $3,792

Extra Principal:

- $1,000

Total Effective Monthly Payment:

- $4,792 plus annual $15,000 lump sums

Results of the Strategy

Instead of taking 30 years to pay off the mortgage, the homeowner could potentially eliminate the loan in approximately:

Approximately 12–13 Years

That means:

- Mortgage paid off about 17–18 years early
- Interest savings potentially exceeding $400,000

The homeowner not only becomes debt-free dramatically faster, but also frees up nearly $3,800 per month years earlier than expected.

Long-Term Wealth Impact

Once the mortgage is eliminated, imagine the homeowner redirects the former mortgage payment of $3,792 monthly into investments earning an average 8% annual return.

Over the next 15 years, that redirected mortgage payment could potentially grow into well over $1 million depending on investment performance and consistency. This demonstrates one of the most important principles in personal finance: Mortgage acceleration is not only about eliminating debt. It is about reclaiming future cash flow earlier so that money can begin building wealth for you instead of building profit for the lender.

A structured payoff system using bonuses, tax refunds, and side income can completely transform a family's long-term financial future.

Chapter 5

The Psychology of Mortgage Freedom and How Debt Impacts Your Life More Than You Realize

Most conversations about mortgage payoff focus heavily on mathematics. People discuss interest savings, amortization schedules, investment comparisons, and payoff timelines. While the numbers are extremely important, there is another side of mortgage debt that many homeowners underestimate: the psychological impact. Carrying large debt obligations affects emotions, stress levels, decision-making, relationships, career choices, confidence, and long-term quality of life in ways many individuals do not fully recognize until the debt begins disappearing.

A mortgage is often considered "good debt" because it finances an appreciating asset and helps families build ownership over time. In many situations, this is true. Homeownership can become an important foundation for long-term wealth. However, even beneficial debt still creates obligation. Obligation creates pressure. And pressure affects behavior whether people consciously acknowledge it or not. Many homeowners normalize mortgage stress because it becomes such a common part of adult life. Monthly payments continue for decades, eventually blending into routine existence. Yet beneath the surface, large financial obligations quietly shape daily decisions. They influence where people work, how much risk they take, whether they start businesses, when they retire, how often they travel, how much they save, and even how they feel emotionally during economic uncertainty.

One of the most significant psychological effects of mortgage debt is reduced flexibility. When homeowners carry large balances and high monthly obligations, they often feel trapped financially. Career decisions become heavily tied to income stability rather than personal fulfillment. Individuals may stay in stressful jobs longer than necessary because they fear losing the ability to make mortgage payments. Entrepreneurs may avoid business opportunities because debt obligations make risk feel too dangerous. Families may delay lifestyle changes, relocation opportunities, or personal goals because fixed monthly obligations dominate financial planning.

Mortgage debt can also create ongoing low-level anxiety that becomes normalized over time. Many homeowners experience stress during economic downturns, housing market shifts, layoffs, business slowdowns, or health emergencies because they know large monthly obligations remain unavoidable regardless of life circumstances. Even financially responsible individuals may carry underlying fear about maintaining long-term payment stability.

As mortgage balances decline, many homeowners experience emotional changes that surprise them. Confidence often increases. Financial fear decreases. Decision-making improves. Long-term planning feels more realistic. Reduced debt creates emotional breathing room that many people have not experienced since before purchasing a home.

One of the most powerful aspects of strategic mortgage reduction is that it creates both mathematical and emotional progress simultaneously. Every principal reduction not only lowers future interest obligations but also increases psychological ownership. The homeowner begins feeling less controlled by debt and more empowered financially.

This emotional momentum matters greatly because behavior often determines financial outcomes more than intelligence alone. Many people know what they should do financially but struggle with consistency because they feel overwhelmed, discouraged, or trapped. Visible mortgage progress changes emotional energy. When homeowners begin seeing balances shrink faster than expected, motivation often increases dramatically. Another major psychological benefit of mortgage reduction is improved sleep and reduced stress. Financial stress is one of the leading causes of anxiety, relationship tension, and emotional exhaustion in many households. Couples frequently argue about money because financial pressure amplifies emotional reactions during difficult periods. As debt declines, many families experience greater emotional stability and less tension surrounding finances.

This is particularly true for households living close to their maximum financial limits. High monthly obligations leave little room for mistakes or unexpected events. Even strong incomes may feel insufficient when large portions are consumed by mortgage payments, taxes, insurance, and debt obligations. Reducing mortgage balances creates increased margin and flexibility within the household budget.

Another overlooked psychological factor involves identity and self-worth. Modern culture often encourages people to associate financial success with visible lifestyle indicators such as large homes, luxury cars, expensive vacations, or upscale spending habits. Unfortunately, many individuals increase debt dramatically in pursuit of appearing successful externally while sacrificing long-term peace internally.

True financial confidence usually comes not from displaying wealth, but from increasing control over obligations. A homeowner with moderate lifestyle expenses and low debt often experiences far greater peace than someone earning significantly more while carrying enormous obligations. Financial freedom is frequently more connected to reduced dependence than increased consumption.

This perspective shifts how homeowners evaluate money over time. Instead of asking, “How much can I afford to buy?” financially mature individuals begin asking, “How much freedom does this decision create or remove from my future?”

Mortgage acceleration often becomes addictive in a positive way because every balance reduction creates emotional reinforcement. Homeowners begin realizing that debt reduction directly improves quality of life. The process transforms from simple financial management into personal empowerment.

Another major psychological transformation occurs when individuals stop viewing their mortgage as permanent. Many people unconsciously assume mortgage debt will simply exist for thirty years because that is the standard structure presented by lenders. Once homeowners begin making strategic lump sum payments and seeing accelerated progress, they realize the timeline is flexible. This realization changes behavior dramatically. Instead of feeling trapped inside a predetermined system, borrowers begin feeling capable of engineering their financial future intentionally. Control replaces helplessness. Momentum replaces stagnation.

There is also a profound emotional difference between mandatory obligations and optional choices. A large mortgage payment is not optional. It must be paid regardless of emotional state, market conditions, or life circumstances. As debt decreases, homeowners gradually reclaim income that can eventually become flexible and self-directed.

This future flexibility becomes incredibly valuable later in life. A homeowner approaching retirement with little or no mortgage debt often experiences far greater security than someone still carrying substantial balances. Reduced obligations lower the amount of income required for stability, which can dramatically improve retirement confidence and lifestyle flexibility.

Parents also frequently experience emotional relief knowing reduced debt creates greater ability to help children financially, support aging family members, or navigate emergencies without panic. Mortgage reduction can strengthen not only individual stability but also multigenerational financial resilience.

Another important psychological concept involves opportunity freedom. Individuals carrying heavy debt often avoid opportunities because the consequences of failure feel too dangerous. A person with minimal obligations may feel comfortable launching a business, changing careers, relocating, investing, or pursuing creative passions. In contrast, someone burdened by massive fixed obligations may feel forced to prioritize immediate stability over long-term growth or fulfillment.

Reduced debt expands life choices.

This does not mean all debt is inherently bad or that every homeowner should aggressively eliminate mortgages at the expense of everything else. Intelligent financial planning still requires balance. Investments, retirement accounts, liquidity, business opportunities, and quality of life remain important. However, understanding the emotional impact of debt allows homeowners to make more intentional decisions aligned with their personal goals and values.

Another critical factor involves financial resilience during economic uncertainty. Markets fluctuate. Industries change. Health emergencies happen. Business cycles rise and fall. Homeowners with lower debt obligations generally navigate uncertainty with significantly less stress because survival requires less monthly income. This resilience creates psychological confidence that extends into many areas of life.

Individuals become less fearful, less reactive, and often more strategic because they no longer operate under constant financial pressure.

Many homeowners eventually realize something profound during the payoff journey: mortgage freedom is not only about money. It is about reclaiming emotional energy. Debt consumes mental attention constantly. Reducing debt frees mental space for creativity, relationships, health, growth, and long-term vision.

This chapter is designed to help homeowners recognize that mortgage payoff is not merely a mathematical exercise. It is a transformation in lifestyle, psychology, and future possibilities. Every strategic principal payment improves not only the balance sheet but also emotional flexibility and long-term peace of mind.

The lender calculates your mortgage mathematically. But you experience it emotionally.

Every reduction in debt decreases future pressure. Every principal payment increases ownership. Every year removed from the mortgage timeline strengthens future freedom. True wealth is not simply measured by income or possessions. In many cases, true wealth is measured by flexibility, peace, resilience, and control over your own life.

Mortgage freedom helps create all four.

How Reducing Mortgage Debt Improves Both Cash Flow and Emotional Flexibility

Let's examine a realistic example of how accelerated mortgage reduction can dramatically improve both financial stability and long-term lifestyle flexibility.

Homeowner Scenario

- Mortgage Balance: $450,000
- Interest Rate: 6.25% Fixed
- Remaining Loan Term: 30 Years
- Monthly Principal & Interest Payment: Approximately $2,770
- Total Remaining Payments Over 30 Years: Approximately $997,200
- Total Remaining Interest: Approximately $547,200

At first glance, the homeowner may simply focus on the monthly payment of $2,770. However, the long-term reality is much larger. Over thirty years, the homeowner would pay more than half a million dollars in future interest if only minimum payments are made.

Now let's examine what happens when the homeowner creates a strategic payoff plan focused on reducing both debt and stress.

The Strategic Plan

The homeowner commits to:

- Applying a $15,000 annual work bonus toward principal
- Applying a $7,000 annual tax refund toward principal
- Adding an extra $800 monthly principal payment

Total Additional Principal Payments

Annual Lump Sums:

- $22,000 annually

Monthly Extra Principal:

- $800 monthly ($9,600 annually)

Total Extra Principal Annually:

- Approximately $31,600

New Effective Monthly Payment

Original Mortgage Payment:

- $2,770

Extra Monthly Principal:

- $800

Effective Monthly Outflow:

- $3,570 plus annual lump sums

Estimated Results

Instead of taking 30 years to eliminate the mortgage, the homeowner could potentially pay off the loan in approximately:

Approximately 11–12 Years

Estimated Interest Savings

Original Projected Interest:

- Approximately $547,200

New Estimated Interest Paid:

- Approximately $180,000–$220,000

Estimated Interest Savings:

Approximately $325,000–$365,000 Saved

Psychological and Lifestyle Impact

Once the mortgage is eliminated nearly 18 years early, the homeowner permanently frees up approximately:

$2,770 Per Month in Required Cash Flow

That means:

- Lower financial stress during economic downturns
- Greater flexibility to change careers or reduce work hours
- Increased retirement confidence
- More investment flexibility
- Reduced anxiety about job loss or emergencies
- Greater ability to travel, help family, or pursue personal goals

Now imagine the homeowner redirects the former mortgage payment into investments for the next 15 years.

If the homeowner invests $2,770 monthly after mortgage payoff with an average annual return of 8%, the investment account could potentially grow into:

Approximately $900,000 to $1.2 Million Over 15 Years

This example demonstrates something extremely important:

Mortgage payoff is not only about removing debt. It is about creating future flexibility, emotional peace, and long-term financial control years earlier than most people ever imagine possible.

Chapter 6

Avoiding the Biggest Mistakes People Make When Paying Off Their Mortgage Early

Paying off a mortgage early can become one of the most powerful financial decisions a homeowner ever makes. Reduced interest costs, increased cash flow, emotional peace, and long-term financial flexibility all create compelling benefits. However, while mortgage acceleration can dramatically improve financial positioning, many homeowners make serious mistakes during the process because they approach payoff emotionally rather than strategically.

Some individuals become so focused on eliminating debt that they unintentionally weaken their financial stability. Others ignore investment opportunities, eliminate liquidity, create unnecessary stress, or make aggressive financial decisions without considering long-term consequences. Mortgage freedom should strengthen a household financially and emotionally—not create vulnerability or imbalance.

Understanding the most common mortgage payoff mistakes allows homeowners to build intelligent strategies that maximize both safety and long-term wealth creation. The goal is not simply to eliminate debt quickly. The goal is to improve overall financial freedom sustainably.

One of the most common mistakes homeowners make is draining emergency savings to make large principal payments. Excitement about mortgage reduction can become emotionally addictive. Some homeowners become obsessed with seeing the balance decline and begin applying nearly every available dollar toward debt. While reducing principal can create major benefits, eliminating liquidity creates risk.

Life is unpredictable. Job losses, medical emergencies, business slowdowns, home repairs, lawsuits, insurance deductibles, vehicle breakdowns, and family emergencies can appear suddenly. Without adequate emergency reserves, homeowners may be forced to rely on high-interest credit cards, personal loans, or retirement account withdrawals during difficult periods.

A strong emergency fund creates financial stability and emotional confidence. Before becoming highly aggressive with mortgage acceleration, homeowners should generally maintain sufficient accessible reserves to cover several months of living expenses. Mortgage payoff should increase peace of mind rather than create fear about unexpected financial events. Another major mistake is ignoring high-interest debt while aggressively paying down low-interest mortgage debt. Not all debt should be prioritized equally. For example, a homeowner carrying credit card balances at 20% interest while paying down a 5% mortgage aggressively may actually be weakening their financial position mathematically.

High-interest debt compounds rapidly and often creates much larger long-term financial damage than lower-rate mortgage debt. In many situations, eliminating high-interest liabilities first creates the strongest financial foundation before accelerating mortgage payoff aggressively.

This principle requires homeowners to evaluate debt strategically rather than emotionally. Mortgage debt may feel psychologically uncomfortable because of its size, but financial prioritization should still consider interest rates, cash flow impact, and overall long-term consequences.

Another common mistake is failing to understand opportunity cost. Every dollar directed toward mortgage reduction is a dollar unavailable for investing, business growth, retirement contributions, or other wealth-building opportunities. This does not mean mortgage payoff is wrong. It simply means homeowners should evaluate alternative uses of capital intelligently. For example, a homeowner with a 3% fixed mortgage rate may have opportunities to invest in retirement accounts, businesses, real estate, or diversified portfolios producing significantly higher long-term returns. In these situations, aggressively paying off the mortgage at the expense of investing could potentially reduce overall wealth accumulation over time.

On the other hand, some homeowners value reduced risk and emotional peace more heavily than maximizing investment growth. Personal finance is not purely mathematical. Emotional comfort, risk tolerance, age, career stability, and personal goals all matter. The key is intentional decision-making rather than blindly following financial trends or internet opinions.

Another major mistake involves becoming "house rich but cash poor." Some homeowners aggressively pay down mortgage debt until most of their wealth becomes trapped inside home equity while accessible cash remains extremely limited. Although home equity increases net worth technically, it is not always immediately liquid or accessible during emergencies.

Liquidity matters.

A homeowner with substantial home equity but no accessible savings may still experience significant stress during emergencies or economic downturns. Balanced financial planning requires both asset growth and cash flow flexibility. Another overlooked mistake is neglecting retirement contributions while pursuing mortgage freedom. Some individuals become so obsessed with debt elimination that they stop investing for retirement during critical compounding years. This can create major long-term opportunity loss.

Retirement investing benefits tremendously from time and compounding growth. Missing years of retirement contributions—especially during younger working years—can significantly reduce future investment growth potential. In many cases, balancing mortgage acceleration with consistent retirement investing creates a healthier long-term strategy than prioritizing one goal completely at the expense of the other.

This balance becomes especially important when employer retirement matching programs are available. Ignoring employer matching contributions while paying down low-interest mortgage debt may result in losing immediate guaranteed investment returns.

Another emotional mistake homeowners make is comparing their financial journey to others. Social media, financial influencers, and success stories often create unrealistic pressure. Some homeowners become discouraged because they cannot make massive lump sum payments or eliminate mortgages within a few years. Mortgage acceleration is highly personal. Every additional principal payment improves financial positioning regardless of size. A homeowner consistently applying smaller amounts over time may still save enormous interest and eliminate years from the loan schedule. Sustainable consistency usually matters more than dramatic short-term intensity.

Perfection is not required for success.

Another dangerous mistake is sacrificing quality of life completely in pursuit of aggressive payoff. Some individuals eliminate all vacations, hobbies, social activities, family experiences, or personal enjoyment while attacking debt relentlessly. Although discipline matters greatly, financial success should improve life rather than create emotional burnout or relationship strain.

Sustainable strategies usually balance long-term goals with present enjoyment. Financial freedom is not only about the future—it is also about maintaining emotional health and meaningful living during the process itself.

Another critical mistake is failing to verify how lenders apply extra payments. Some homeowners assume additional payments automatically reduce principal when, in reality, certain lenders may apply funds differently unless instructions are clearly specified. Homeowners should confirm that extra payments are designated specifically toward principal reduction rather than future scheduled payments.

Small administrative misunderstandings can reduce the effectiveness of acceleration strategies significantly over time.

Interest rate misunderstandings also create confusion for many homeowners. Some individuals assume all debt should always be eliminated immediately regardless of interest rate environment. Others assume debt should never be paid off because investing always produces higher returns. Both extreme perspectives oversimplify complex financial realities.

A homeowner carrying a high mortgage interest rate during uncertain economic conditions may prioritize aggressive payoff heavily. Another homeowner with a historically low fixed rate and strong investment opportunities may choose a more balanced strategy. Intelligent financial planning considers multiple variables rather than relying on simplistic universal rules.

Tax considerations can also influence mortgage payoff decisions. Mortgage interest deductions, investment tax advantages, business opportunities, and retirement contribution strategies all affect long-term outcomes.

Homeowners should evaluate how mortgage acceleration fits into broader financial planning rather than viewing the mortgage in isolation. Another overlooked mistake is ignoring emotional behavior patterns. Many individuals underestimate how strongly emotions influence financial decisions. Large windfalls, bonuses, inheritance money, or business profits often trigger impulsive spending because people feel emotionally rewarded after financial success.

Without predetermined systems, temporary financial opportunities frequently disappear quickly into lifestyle inflation. Strategic homeowners often create clear allocation plans before receiving windfalls to reduce emotional decision-making. Automation, percentage-based systems, and structured financial rules strengthen discipline significantly.

Many homeowners also fail to celebrate progress properly. Mortgage payoff journeys often last years, and long-term goals can feel emotionally exhausting without positive reinforcement. Celebrating milestones responsibly helps maintain motivation and emotional momentum.

For example, homeowners may recognize every $50,000 reduction in principal or each five-year reduction in projected payoff timeline. Structured milestones help transform mortgage acceleration into a motivating process rather than a never-ending obligation.

Another important lesson is understanding that mortgage freedom itself is not the final destination. Some individuals become so focused on eliminating debt that they fail to build broader long-term wealth systems simultaneously. Mortgage payoff creates opportunity, but homeowners should also develop investing habits, cash flow management, retirement planning, and wealth-building strategies beyond debt elimination.

The ultimate goal is not simply becoming debt-free. The deeper objective is achieving long-term flexibility, resilience, ownership, and financial independence.

One of the most powerful realizations homeowners experience is that financial success is usually built through repeated intelligent decisions rather than dramatic one-time events. Consistent disciplined behavior often matters far more than perfect timing or extreme sacrifice.

Mortgage acceleration works best when integrated into a balanced long-term financial plan that includes emergency reserves, investing, retirement planning, income growth, and healthy lifestyle management.

The homeowners who achieve lasting financial peace are rarely the ones making reckless emotional decisions. Instead, they are usually individuals who build sustainable systems, remain patient, adapt strategically, and consistently align financial behavior with long-term goals.

Mortgage payoff can absolutely become life-changing. But the process should strengthen your life financially, emotionally, and strategically—not weaken it.

True financial wisdom comes not from moving the fastest, but from moving intelligently.

Comparing a Balanced Mortgage Payoff Strategy vs. an Aggressive but Risky Strategy

Let's examine two homeowners with identical mortgage situations but very different payoff approaches.

Mortgage Details for Both Homeowners

- Mortgage Balance: $500,000
- Interest Rate: 5.75% Fixed
- Remaining Loan Term: 30 Years
- Monthly Principal & Interest Payment: Approximately $2,917

- Total Remaining Interest Over 30 Years: Approximately $550,120

Now let's compare two different payoff strategies.

Homeowner A: The Overly Aggressive Strategy

Homeowner A becomes obsessed with paying off the mortgage as fast as possible.

Actions:

- Uses nearly all savings toward principal reduction
- Keeps only $2,000 emergency reserves
- Stops retirement investing completely
- Redirects every bonus and side income payment toward the mortgage
- Makes extra principal payments totaling $4,000 monthly

Results

- Mortgage paid off in approximately 8 years
- Interest savings: approximately $350,000+

At first glance, this appears extremely successful.

However, during year 5:

- Homeowner loses employment during an economic downturn
- Emergency reserves are insufficient
- Retirement contributions have been missed for years
- Homeowner must rely on credit cards and retirement withdrawals for survival

Although the mortgage balance is much lower, financial stress becomes severe because liquidity disappeared.

Homeowner B: The Balanced Strategic Approach

Homeowner B also wants early mortgage freedom but prioritizes balance and resilience.

Actions:

- Maintains 12 months of emergency savings
- Continues maximizing retirement contributions with employer matching
- Invests consistently every month
- Applies:

  - $15,000 annual bonuses toward principal
  - $800 extra monthly principal payments
  - 50% of side hustle income toward the mortgage

Results

- Mortgage paid off in approximately 14–15 years
- Interest savings: approximately $250,000+
- Retirement accounts continue compounding simultaneously
- Emergency fund remains intact during economic uncertainty

Long-Term Wealth Comparison

By retirement age, Homeowner B may actually have:

- Higher total investment assets
- Strong emergency reserves
- Lower stress during downturns
- Significant mortgage interest savings
- Greater overall flexibility

Meanwhile, Homeowner A achieved faster payoff but experienced:

- Financial instability during emergencies
- Lost retirement compounding years
- Increased emotional stress during income disruption

The Key Lesson

Mortgage payoff speed alone does not determine financial success.

The strongest strategy is usually:

- Sustainable
- Balanced
- Emotionally manageable
- Protective during emergencies
- Aligned with long-term investing and wealth-building goals

Intelligent financial planning balances debt reduction with wealth creation instead of focusing blindly on only one objective.

Mortgage freedom should create security and flexibility—not financial fragility.

Chapter 7

Combining Lump Sum Payments with Monthly Extra Payments for Maximum Mortgage Acceleration

One of the most powerful strategies homeowners can use to eliminate mortgage debt faster is combining consistent monthly extra payments with periodic lump sum principal reductions. Many homeowners mistakenly believe they must choose between one strategy or the other. In reality, the greatest mortgage acceleration often occurs when both approaches work together simultaneously. Monthly extra payments create steady momentum while lump sum contributions produce dramatic balance reductions during key moments throughout the life of the loan.

This combination strategy works because it attacks mortgage interest from multiple directions at the same time. Small monthly principal additions reduce the balance consistently every month, while larger lump sum payments interrupt the amortization schedule aggressively whenever temporary income opportunities appear. Together, these methods can reduce decades of debt into significantly shorter payoff timelines while saving enormous amounts in future interest.

Most homeowners already understand the concept of making extra monthly payments. Even adding relatively small amounts toward principal each month can create meaningful long-term savings because the additional funds reduce future interest accumulation continuously. For example, adding just a few hundred dollars monthly toward principal can eliminate years from a mortgage over time.

However, many people underestimate the power of combining these steady payments with strategic lump sums. A homeowner who consistently makes extra monthly payments while also applying bonuses, tax refunds, side income, or investment gains toward principal often creates accelerated results that compound dramatically over time.

The key reason this strategy becomes so effective is that mortgage interest is calculated based on the remaining unpaid balance. Every reduction in principal lowers future interest calculations permanently. Monthly extra payments gradually weaken the lender's interest position every month, while lump sum payments create larger immediate reductions that accelerate future savings even more aggressively.

The earlier these combined payments occur in the life of the loan, the greater the long-term impact often becomes. During the early years of a mortgage, lenders collect a substantial portion of their profits through interest-heavy payments. Strategic principal reductions during this period interrupt decades of future interest accumulation before it has time to compound fully.

While many borrowers simply accept the lender's schedule as fixed, financially disciplined homeowners recognize that every extra principal payment changes the equation. By reducing the principal balance aggressively and consistently, homeowners alter the trajectory of the loan entirely.

Another major advantage of combining monthly and lump sum strategies is psychological reinforcement. Mortgage payoff can sometimes feel slow when relying only on occasional large payments or only on modest monthly additions. Combining both approaches creates visible momentum more frequently. Monthly progress keeps motivation alive while periodic lump sums create major breakthroughs that reinforce discipline emotionally.

This momentum matters because financial success is often behavioral rather than purely mathematical. Many homeowners begin mortgage acceleration enthusiastically but lose motivation over time when progress feels invisible. Seeing consistent balance reductions helps maintain emotional engagement and strengthens long-term discipline. One highly effective approach involves establishing a fixed monthly extra payment amount based on stable income while using irregular income streams for lump sum acceleration. For example, a homeowner may consistently add $500 monthly toward principal while directing annual bonuses, tax refunds, side business income, or commissions toward larger principal reductions throughout the year.

This structure creates both consistency and flexibility.

The monthly extra payment becomes part of the normal household budget, while lump sums allow homeowners to capitalize on temporary financial opportunities without relying entirely on unpredictable income sources.

Another advantage of combining strategies is adaptability during different life stages. Some years may produce larger bonuses or windfalls, while other years may involve tighter budgets. Monthly extra payments can provide steady progress even during slower financial periods, while larger lump sums accelerate payoff during stronger income years.

Homeowners should also recognize that even modest combinations can create dramatic long-term results. Many individuals assume they need extremely high incomes or enormous windfalls to pay off a mortgage early. In reality, consistent smaller actions repeated over long periods often produce extraordinary outcomes.

For example, adding an extra $500 monthly while applying one annual $10,000 bonus toward principal every year can potentially eliminate many years from a standard mortgage. The combined effect becomes increasingly powerful because every early reduction lowers future interest obligations permanently.

Automation can strengthen this strategy significantly. Many homeowners set up automatic monthly extra principal payments directly through their lender while manually applying lump sums during bonus periods or windfall events. Automation reduces emotional inconsistency and helps maintain discipline even during busy or stressful seasons of life.

Another important factor involves lifestyle management. The most successful homeowners usually avoid allowing rising income to fully inflate lifestyle expenses. Instead of automatically increasing spending after raises or bonuses, they intentionally allocate portions toward long-term financial improvement. Mortgage acceleration becomes part of a broader philosophy of intentional wealth building rather than reactive consumption.

This mindset shift often separates financially free individuals from those who remain trapped despite high incomes. Income alone rarely creates wealth automatically. Strategic allocation decisions create wealth.

Another major advantage of combining payoff strategies is risk reduction over time. Every principal reduction lowers future obligations. As balances decline faster, homeowners gradually become less financially vulnerable during economic downturns, business slowdowns, or career transitions. Reduced debt increases flexibility and resilience simultaneously.

Many homeowners also discover that mortgage acceleration changes their relationship with money itself. Instead of viewing extra income purely as spending power, they begin seeing it as a tool for increasing future freedom. Every extra payment becomes an investment in lower future obligations and greater long-term control over life decisions.

This perspective creates emotional maturity around financial planning. Temporary sacrifices begin feeling purposeful rather than restrictive because homeowners can see measurable progress toward meaningful goals.

Another important concept is compounding momentum. Mortgage acceleration often feels modest initially because balances remain large during early stages. However, as balances shrink and interest accumulation weakens, payoff progress frequently accelerates more dramatically. The combination of steady monthly reductions and recurring lump sums creates increasing momentum over time.

Homeowners should also periodically review and adjust their payoff strategies as life changes. Income growth, career shifts, investment opportunities, family responsibilities, and economic conditions may all influence how aggressively mortgage reduction should be prioritized during different periods.

For example, younger homeowners with strong investment opportunities and low mortgage rates may balance investing and payoff more evenly. Later in life, as retirement approaches, some homeowners may prioritize aggressive mortgage elimination more heavily to reduce future obligations.

Flexibility remains important because financial planning is dynamic rather than static.

Another overlooked advantage of accelerated payoff is future cash flow liberation. Every year removed from the mortgage timeline represents years of future income no longer committed to mandatory debt payments. Once the mortgage disappears, former mortgage payments can be redirected toward investing, business ownership, retirement accounts, travel, philanthropy, or lifestyle flexibility. This future cash flow transformation can become life-changing.

A homeowner paying $3,000 monthly toward a mortgage who eliminates the loan fifteen years early effectively frees up over half a million dollars in future payment obligations before even considering investment growth opportunities afterward.

Mortgage acceleration also creates emotional confidence during uncertain economic environments. Individuals carrying lower debt often feel calmer and more strategic because survival requires less monthly income. Reduced obligations lower pressure and increase freedom simultaneously.

One of the most important lessons homeowners eventually learn is that consistency usually matters more than intensity. Some individuals make one large lump sum payment and then abandon the process entirely. Others attempt extremely aggressive payoff plans that become emotionally exhausting and financially unsustainable.

Balanced consistency typically produces stronger long-term results.

Homeowners who combine manageable monthly extra payments with strategic lump sums often create sustainable systems that continue for years without burnout. Small disciplined actions repeated consistently frequently outperform emotionally extreme strategies that collapse quickly. This chapter is designed to help homeowners understand that mortgage acceleration does not require perfection, extreme deprivation, or unrealistic income levels. Instead, meaningful progress usually comes from combining intelligent systems with repeated disciplined behavior over time.

Every extra monthly payment weakens future interest accumulation. Every lump sum reduction accelerates momentum further. Together, these actions compound into major financial transformation.

Mortgage freedom is rarely the result of one giant financial event alone. More often, it is built gradually through repeated strategic decisions aligned with long-term goals.

The homeowners who achieve extraordinary financial progress are often not the ones earning the most money. Frequently, they are the individuals who consistently direct temporary financial opportunities toward permanent improvements.

Every additional principal payment—whether large or small—moves the homeowner closer to greater freedom, flexibility, and long-term financial independence.

Combining Monthly Extra Payments and Annual Lump Sums

Let's examine how combining consistent monthly extra payments with annual lump sum contributions can dramatically accelerate mortgage payoff.

Mortgage Details

- Mortgage Amount: $550,000
- Interest Rate: 6.0% Fixed
- Loan Term: 30 Years
- Monthly Principal & Interest Payment: Approximately $3,298
- Total Payments Over 30 Years: Approximately $1,187,280
- Total Interest Paid: Approximately $637,280

Now let's compare different payoff approaches.

Scenario 1: Minimum Payments Only

If the homeowner simply follows the standard 30-year schedule:

- Mortgage payoff timeline: 30 years
- Total interest paid: approximately $637,280

The lender collects more than half a million dollars in interest over the life of the loan.

Scenario 2: Adding Only $500 Extra Monthly

The homeowner decides to add:

- $500 extra principal monthly

New effective monthly payment:

- $3,798 monthly

Estimated Results

- Mortgage payoff timeline reduced to approximately 21–22 years
- Interest savings: approximately $180,000–$220,000

Even a relatively modest monthly increase creates major long-term savings.

Scenario 3: Combining Monthly Extra Payments PLUS Annual Lump Sums

Now the homeowner combines:

- $500 extra monthly principal
- $15,000 annual work bonus toward principal
- $5,000 annual tax refund toward principal

Total Extra Contributions

- Monthly extra payments: $6,000 annually
- Annual lump sums: $20,000 annually
- Total extra principal annually: approximately $26,000

Estimated Results

Instead of taking 30 years to eliminate the mortgage:

The mortgage could potentially be paid off in approximately 11–13 years

Estimated Interest Savings

Original Interest:

- Approximately $637,280

New Estimated Interest:

- Approximately $200,000–$240,000

Estimated Interest Saved

Approximately $400,000+ Saved

Future Cash Flow Freedom

Once the mortgage is eliminated nearly 18 years early:

- The homeowner permanently frees up approximately $3,298 monthly

If that former mortgage payment is invested for the following 15 years at an average annual return of 8%, the results could become extraordinary.

By investing the former mortgage payment consistently:

- Potential future investment value could exceed $1 million depending on timing and returns.

Key Lesson

This example demonstrates the hidden power of combining strategies.

Small consistent monthly extra payments create steady momentum. Annual lump sums create dramatic acceleration. Together, they can completely transform a homeowner's long-term financial future.

Mortgage acceleration is often not about one giant payment alone. It is about building a repeatable system where every financial opportunity—large or small—is used intentionally to create long-term freedom.

Chapter 8

Building Long-Term Wealth After Your Mortgage Is Paid Off

For many homeowners, the idea of paying off a mortgage early represents the ultimate financial finish line. They imagine the final payment, the release of the lien, and the emotional relief that comes from finally owning the home free and clear. While this achievement is incredibly powerful, financially intelligent homeowners understand something even more important: paying off the mortgage is not the end of the wealth-building journey. In many ways, it is the beginning of an entirely new phase of financial opportunity.

The moment a mortgage disappears, one of the largest monthly obligations in most households vanishes permanently. Thousands of dollars that were previously committed to debt service every month suddenly become available for investing, business ownership, real estate expansion, retirement acceleration, lifestyle flexibility, family support, philanthropy, or long-term wealth creation. This transition can completely transform a household's financial trajectory if handled strategically. Many people spend so many years focused on paying off debt that they fail to prepare for what comes afterward. Without intentional planning, some homeowners simply replace old debt obligations with new spending habits. The financial freedom created by mortgage elimination can quietly disappear through lifestyle inflation, unnecessary purchases, or poorly structured financial decisions. True long-term wealth comes not merely from eliminating debt, but from redirecting freed cash flow intentionally toward assets that continue generating future income and financial growth.

One of the most important mindset shifts homeowners must develop is understanding the difference between consumption and wealth creation. Consumption removes cash flow permanently in exchange for temporary lifestyle satisfaction. Wealth creation redirects cash flow into assets that continue producing value over time. Once the mortgage is eliminated, homeowners gain a rare opportunity to dramatically increase the percentage of income flowing toward wealth-building rather than debt obligations.

For example, a homeowner previously paying $3,500 monthly toward a mortgage suddenly gains the ability to redirect over $42,000 annually toward investments or other financial goals once the loan disappears. Over time, this shift can create extraordinary compounding wealth.

Once mortgage obligations disappear, homeowners can redirect former debt payments into appreciating assets that compound positively over time rather than continuing to transfer interest payments to lenders. This transition marks a major turning point in long-term wealth building.

One of the simplest and most effective post-mortgage strategies involves aggressive investing. Homeowners who redirect former mortgage payments into retirement accounts, index funds, dividend investments, real estate acquisitions, or business opportunities can potentially build substantial wealth far faster than during their debt-heavy years. The psychological difference is also important because investing after debt reduction often feels emotionally easier and less stressful.

Many homeowners experience tremendous relief knowing their housing security no longer depends on large monthly obligations. This emotional confidence often improves long-term investment discipline because individuals feel less financially vulnerable during market volatility or economic uncertainty.

Another major benefit of mortgage elimination is increased career flexibility. Many individuals remain tied to high-stress jobs primarily because large monthly obligations require stable income continuously. Once the mortgage disappears, homeowners often gain the freedom to pursue more meaningful work, reduce working hours, launch businesses, consult independently, or transition toward semi-retirement lifestyles.

Reduced obligations create options.

This flexibility becomes increasingly valuable later in life when priorities often shift from maximizing income toward maximizing quality of life, health, family time, and personal fulfillment.

Another powerful strategy after mortgage payoff involves acquiring additional cash-flowing assets. Some homeowners use their newly liberated cash flow to purchase rental properties, invest in businesses, or expand real estate portfolios. Instead of allowing lifestyle inflation to absorb the freed monthly income, they intentionally convert debt-free cash flow into additional income-producing assets.

This creates a compounding wealth cycle. Assets begin generating cash flow, which can then fund additional investments or lifestyle flexibility without relying entirely on employment income.

For example, a homeowner who redirects a former $3,000

mortgage payment toward acquiring rental real estate may eventually create enough passive income to cover living expenses entirely. At that point, financial independence becomes increasingly realistic because cash flow comes from assets rather than only active labor.

Another important concept is risk reduction. A debt-free home dramatically improves financial resilience during uncertain economic periods. Recessions, layoffs, business disruptions, market volatility, and health emergencies become significantly less threatening when housing obligations are minimal or eliminated entirely.

Many retirees especially recognize the importance of this stability. A homeowner entering retirement without a mortgage often requires substantially less income to maintain lifestyle stability. This lowers dependence on investment withdrawals and increases retirement sustainability significantly.

Healthcare costs, inflation, and longevity risks all create uncertainty later in life. Reduced housing obligations provide critical financial breathing room during these periods. Many retirees discover that a paid-off home becomes one of their strongest financial protections.

Another often-overlooked benefit of mortgage freedom is emotional energy. Debt consumes mental attention constantly. Monthly obligations create background stress that many individuals normalize over time. Once major debt disappears, homeowners frequently experience increased clarity, creativity, optimism, and confidence.

This emotional shift can influence many areas of life including health, relationships, business decisions, and long-term planning. Financial freedom is not merely about money—it is about reducing pressure and increasing control over personal choices.

However, another major mistake homeowners sometimes make after mortgage payoff is becoming overly conservative financially. Some individuals stop investing aggressively because they feel emotionally secure once the house is paid off. While reduced debt creates stability, long-term wealth still requires growth-oriented behavior.

Inflation continues regardless of mortgage status. A debt-free homeowner who stops investing may still struggle financially decades later if assets fail to grow appropriately over time. Mortgage elimination should become the foundation for future wealth creation rather than the endpoint of financial planning entirely.

Balance remains important.

Some homeowners prioritize conservative investing and stability after mortgage payoff. Others pursue aggressive asset accumulation. Some focus on travel and lifestyle freedom. Others transition toward entrepreneurship or family legacy planning. The best strategy depends on age, goals, health, risk tolerance, and personal values.

Another important concept involves multigenerational wealth. A paid-off home often becomes one of the largest assets families pass to future generations. Reduced debt allows families to allocate more resources toward education, investing, businesses, trusts, or long-term family support structures.

Parents with reduced financial pressure often gain greater ability to help children responsibly without sacrificing retirement security themselves. Financial flexibility expands not only for the individual homeowner but potentially for future generations as well.

Another overlooked opportunity after mortgage payoff is charitable giving and impact creation. Some individuals discover that once major debt disappears, they finally gain the flexibility to support causes, organizations, communities, or family members in ways previously impossible. Financial freedom creates increased capacity for generosity.

One of the most powerful lessons homeowners eventually learn is that wealth is not simply measured by income levels. Many high-income earners remain financially trapped because obligations consume most of their cash flow continuously. In contrast, individuals with lower obligations often experience far greater freedom despite earning less. This is why mortgage elimination can feel so transformative emotionally. It reduces dependence.

Once basic housing security no longer requires large monthly debt service, the homeowner's relationship with money changes dramatically. Income becomes increasingly optional rather than entirely mandatory for survival.

Another important post-payoff strategy involves maintaining disciplined financial habits even after the mortgage disappears. Some homeowners become careless once the debt is eliminated, increasing spending dramatically or taking on unnecessary new liabilities. Long-term wealth requires continued intentionality even after major financial goals are achieved.

The homeowners who build lasting financial freedom are usually those who continue directing significant portions of income toward appreciating assets, investments, businesses, or future-oriented planning rather than allowing consumption to dominate financial behavior again.

Mortgage payoff also creates opportunities for accelerated retirement planning. Without housing debt, retirement contribution capacity often increases substantially. Former mortgage payments can be redirected toward tax-advantaged retirement accounts, brokerage investments, or passive income assets aggressively during the final working years before retirement.

This acceleration can dramatically improve long-term financial independence.

The transition from debt repayment to asset accumulation marks one of the most important financial turning points in a person's life. For years, homeowners direct income toward eliminating obligations. After payoff, that same income can begin building ownership, investments, and long-term freedom instead.

This chapter is designed to help homeowners understand that mortgage freedom is not the finish line—it is a launch point. Eliminating mortgage debt creates opportunities far beyond simple monthly payment relief. It creates flexibility, resilience, confidence, and long-term wealth-building potential.

Every principal payment made during the payoff journey was not merely reducing debt. It was gradually reclaiming future cash flow and future choice.

The ultimate goal is not simply to own a home free and clear. The deeper goal is to create a life where financial decisions are increasingly guided by purpose, freedom, and opportunity rather than obligation.

Mortgage freedom creates the space for that transformation to begin.

Turning a Paid-Off Mortgage into Long-Term Wealth

Let's examine how paying off a mortgage early can dramatically increase long-term wealth when the former mortgage payment is redirected strategically.

Homeowner Scenario

- Mortgage Amount: $600,000
- Interest Rate: 6.25% Fixed
- Original Loan Term: 30 Years
- Monthly Principal & Interest Payment: Approximately $3,694

- Total Interest Over 30 Years: Approximately $729,840

The homeowner aggressively combines:

- Extra monthly principal payments
- Annual bonuses
- Tax refunds
- Side hustle income

As a result, the mortgage is paid off in approximately:

13 Years Instead of 30 Years

Interest Savings

Original Projected Interest:

- Approximately $729,840

Actual Interest Paid:

- Approximately $250,000–$300,000

Estimated Interest Saved:

Approximately $430,000–$480,000 Saved

Now let's examine the true long-term opportunity.

What Happens After the Mortgage Is Gone?

The homeowner now has:

- No mortgage payment
- An additional $3,694 monthly cash flow available

Instead of increasing lifestyle spending dramatically, the homeowner decides to invest the former mortgage payment consistently.

Investment Assumptions

- Monthly Investment: $3,694
- Average Annual Return: 8%
- Investment Period: 17 Years (the years saved by paying off early)

Potential Investment Growth

By investing the former mortgage payment for the remaining 17 years:

Potential Future Investment Value:

Approximately $1.6 Million to $2 Million+

This example demonstrates an incredibly important principle:

Paying off a mortgage early does not only save interest.

It also creates the opportunity to redirect massive monthly cash flow into appreciating assets years earlier than normal.

Additional Benefits Beyond the Numbers

The homeowner also gains:

- Greater retirement flexibility
- Lower financial stress
- Reduced dependence on employment income
- Increased emergency resilience
- More freedom to pursue business or investment opportunities
- Greater ability to help family or future generations
- Increased confidence during economic downturns

The Key Lesson

Mortgage payoff is not simply about becoming debt-free.

It is about reclaiming future income and redirecting it toward wealth creation instead of lender profit.

The earlier homeowners eliminate major obligations, the earlier they gain the power to let compounding investments begin working fully in their favor.

Chapter 9

Creating Your Personal Mortgage Payoff Blueprint for Long-Term Financial Freedom

Every homeowner's financial situation is different. Income levels, career stability, family responsibilities, interest rates, investment goals, risk tolerance, and lifestyle priorities all vary significantly from person to person. Because of this, there is no single perfect mortgage payoff strategy that works universally for everyone. The homeowners who achieve the greatest long-term success are usually not the ones blindly copying someone else's plan. Instead, they are the individuals who create personalized mortgage payoff blueprints aligned with their unique financial reality and long-term vision for life.

A mortgage payoff blueprint is more than simply deciding to make extra payments. It is a structured long-term financial system designed to reduce debt intentionally while balancing investing, cash flow management, lifestyle goals, emergency preparedness, and future wealth creation. Without a blueprint, homeowners often drift financially, making random decisions based on emotion rather than long-term strategy. With a blueprint, every financial action becomes connected to a larger vision of freedom and stability.

One of the first steps in creating a personal mortgage payoff blueprint is identifying your ultimate financial goal. Many homeowners say they want to pay off their mortgage early, but few clearly define why. Understanding the deeper reason behind the goal is extremely important because motivation strengthens when financial goals connect to meaningful life outcomes.

For some individuals, the primary goal is reducing stress and increasing peace of mind. Others want retirement security. Some desire career flexibility or entrepreneurship opportunities. Others want to build long-term wealth faster, eliminate financial pressure from their family, or create multigenerational stability. Some homeowners simply want the emotional satisfaction of complete ownership.

The clearer the emotional purpose behind the strategy, the easier it becomes to maintain discipline during difficult periods.

Another important step is understanding your current financial foundation honestly. Before aggressively accelerating mortgage payoff, homeowners should evaluate several critical areas:

- Emergency savings
- High-interest debt
- Retirement contributions
- Monthly cash flow stability
- Insurance protection
- Career stability
- Investment opportunities
- Family obligations

Mortgage acceleration works best when built on top of a stable financial foundation rather than on top of financial chaos. A homeowner struggling with credit card debt, unstable income, or no emergency reserves may need a more balanced strategy initially compared to someone with strong cash flow and significant savings.

Once the foundation is understood clearly, homeowners should analyze the mortgage itself in detail. Important factors include:

- Remaining balance
- Interest rate

- Remaining loan term
- Monthly payment amount
- Total projected future interest
- Loan type
- Refinancing opportunities
- Prepayment flexibility

Many homeowners become significantly more motivated after reviewing the true long-term interest cost of their loan. Seeing the actual projected lender profit often creates urgency around principal reduction and long-term planning.

Every principal reduction changes future interest calculations and shortens the financial timeline. Understanding this system empowers homeowners to create strategies intentionally instead of simply accepting the lender's original schedule passively.

The next step in building a blueprint involves selecting the combination of acceleration strategies that best fit your personality and financial structure. Some homeowners prefer aggressive monthly extra payments because consistency feels easier psychologically. Others rely heavily on annual lump sums from bonuses, commissions, tax refunds, or business profits. Many successful homeowners combine multiple strategies simultaneously.

For example, one homeowner may choose:

- $500 extra monthly principal payments
- 50% of annual bonuses toward principal
- 100% of tax refunds toward principal
- Side hustle income dedicated to mortgage reduction

Another homeowner may prioritize investing heavily while making moderate extra payments due to low mortgage interest rates and strong retirement goals. A business owner may use fluctuating income strategically during strong revenue periods while maintaining flexibility during slower seasons.

There is no perfect universal structure. The strongest blueprint is usually the one that remains emotionally sustainable for many years.

Sustainability matters tremendously because mortgage payoff is typically a long-term process rather than a short-term sprint. Some homeowners begin with unrealistic intensity and eventually burn out emotionally. Others become discouraged because they expect dramatic results too quickly. Consistent sustainable behavior usually creates stronger long-term outcomes than emotionally extreme approaches. Automation can strengthen almost every payoff blueprint. Human behavior is naturally inconsistent during stressful or busy periods. Automatic principal payments, scheduled transfers, and predefined allocation systems reduce emotional decision-making and help maintain discipline over time.

For example, homeowners may automate:

- Monthly extra principal payments
- Bonus allocation percentages
- Side income transfers
- Investment contributions
- Emergency savings deposits

Automation transforms good intentions into repeatable financial systems.

Another critical component of a strong blueprint is periodic review and adjustment. Life changes continuously. Careers evolve, families grow, markets shift, and opportunities appear unexpectedly. A mortgage payoff plan should remain flexible enough to adapt intelligently over time.

For example:

- A homeowner receiving a major promotion may accelerate payoff aggressively.
- Someone approaching retirement may prioritize eliminating obligations more heavily.
- A business owner during uncertain economic conditions may temporarily increase liquidity reserves instead of making large lump sums.
- An investor may rebalance between mortgage reduction and investment opportunities depending on market conditions.

Financial planning should evolve with life circumstances rather than remain rigid permanently.

Another powerful aspect of building a blueprint is tracking measurable progress. Homeowners who monitor their payoff timeline, balance reductions, interest savings, and equity growth often maintain stronger motivation than those operating blindly. Visible progress reinforces disciplined behavior emotionally.

Some homeowners create milestone goals such as:

- Reducing the balance below certain thresholds
- Eliminating five years from the payoff timeline
- Reaching 50% equity ownership
- Saving a targeted amount in interest

Milestones transform mortgage payoff into a visible journey rather than an abstract long-term obligation.

Another important part of a payoff blueprint involves balancing present enjoyment with future freedom. Financial discipline should improve life rather than create constant deprivation. Some individuals become so obsessed with debt elimination that they sacrifice relationships, health, experiences, or emotional well-being unnecessarily.

The purpose of mortgage freedom is ultimately to create a better life—not simply a smaller loan balance.

Healthy financial planning usually includes room for meaningful experiences, family time, travel, hobbies, generosity, and emotional well-being alongside disciplined wealth-building behavior.

Another essential lesson is understanding that financial freedom is deeply connected to cash flow control. Many people focus excessively on net worth while ignoring monthly obligations. A household earning substantial income may still feel trapped if large portions of cash flow remain committed to debt continuously.

Reducing mortgage obligations improves flexibility dramatically because it lowers the minimum income required for stability. This creates optionality in nearly every area of life. Career choices expand. Investment flexibility increases. Retirement becomes more realistic. Business opportunities feel less risky. Stress often declines significantly.

Another powerful concept involves future identity. Homeowners should periodically ask themselves:

- What kind of financial life do I want ten years from now?
- How much flexibility do I want?
- What would life look like without mortgage pressure?
- What opportunities would become possible?

These questions help align daily financial behavior with long-term vision.

The homeowners who successfully eliminate mortgages early often think differently from average consumers. They stop viewing money only through the lens of spending and begin viewing it through the lens of freedom, ownership, leverage, and future opportunity. Every financial decision becomes connected to a larger strategy rather than temporary emotional satisfaction.

Another important part of the blueprint involves post-payoff planning. Many individuals focus so heavily on eliminating debt that they never prepare for what comes afterward. Yet the years immediately following mortgage payoff often become some of the most financially powerful years of a person's life because former mortgage payments can now flow directly toward wealth creation.

Homeowners should already have a vision for how future freed cash flow will be used:

- Investing
- Retirement acceleration
- Business ownership
- Real estate acquisition
- Family support

- Travel
- Passive income development
- Charitable giving
- Lifestyle flexibility

Mortgage freedom creates opportunity, but intentional planning determines whether that opportunity becomes lasting wealth.

Another key lesson is patience. Financial transformation rarely occurs overnight. Mortgage acceleration works through compounding consistency over time. Every extra principal payment creates permanent improvement even when progress initially feels slow. Momentum gradually builds, and eventually the payoff process often accelerates faster than expected.

Homeowners who remain disciplined during ordinary months often create extraordinary results over decades.

This chapter is designed to help homeowners move beyond random financial behavior and toward intentional long-term planning. A personalized mortgage payoff blueprint transforms debt reduction from a vague goal into a measurable actionable strategy aligned with your life vision.

The most financially successful homeowners are rarely the luckiest. More often, they are the individuals who consistently make intentional decisions aligned with long-term goals while remaining flexible, disciplined, and emotionally balanced.

Mortgage freedom is not built accidentally.

It is engineered through repeated intentional choices over time.

Building a Personalized Mortgage Payoff Blueprint

Let's examine a realistic example of how a homeowner can build a personalized mortgage payoff strategy based on income structure, goals, and financial balance.

Homeowner Scenario

Profile

- Age: 40
- Married with two children
- Combined Household Income: $220,000 annually
- Stable salaried employment plus side business income

Mortgage Details

- Remaining Mortgage Balance: $520,000
- Interest Rate: 5.9% Fixed
- Remaining Loan Term: 28 Years
- Monthly Principal & Interest Payment: Approximately $3,090
- Total Remaining Interest if Minimum Payments Continue: Approximately $518,000

At first glance, the mortgage appears manageable because the household earns a strong income. However, the homeowners realize they could potentially pay over half a million dollars in future interest if they follow the original schedule.

Instead of making random extra payments occasionally, they decide to build a complete mortgage payoff blueprint.

Their Strategic Blueprint

Step 1: Maintain Financial Stability

Before accelerating aggressively, they:

- Maintain 12 months of emergency savings

- Continue maximizing retirement contributions
- Eliminate remaining credit card balances
- Keep adequate insurance coverage

This creates a stable financial foundation.

Step 2: Monthly Extra Principal Payments

The homeowners commit to:

- $1,000 extra principal monthly

New effective monthly payment:

- Approximately $4,090 monthly

Step 3: Annual Lump Sum Contributions

They also commit to:

- $12,000 annual work bonuses toward principal
- $8,000 annual side business profits toward principal
- $5,000 tax refund toward principal

Total annual lump sums:

- $25,000 annually

Step 4: Progress Tracking

They review:

- Mortgage balance quarterly
- Updated payoff timeline annually
- Interest savings progress yearly

This keeps motivation strong.

Results of the Blueprint

Instead of paying off the mortgage in 28 years:

Estimated New Payoff Timeline:

Approximately 11–13 Years

Estimated Interest Paid:

- Approximately $180,000–$230,000

Estimated Interest Savings:

Approximately $300,000+ Saved

Post-Payoff Wealth Opportunity

Once the mortgage disappears nearly 15+ years early:

- The homeowners free up approximately $3,090 monthly permanently

If they redirect that former mortgage payment into investments earning an average annual return of 8% for the next 15 years:

Potential Future Investment Growth:

Approximately $1 Million+ Over 15 Years

Additional Lifestyle Benefits

Beyond the numbers, the homeowners also gain:

- Reduced financial stress
- Greater career flexibility
- Increased retirement confidence
- Lower dependence on employment income
- Improved resilience during economic downturns
- More options for travel, investing, and family support

Key Lesson

The power of a mortgage payoff blueprint comes from structure and consistency.

The homeowners did not rely on luck, inheritance money, or unrealistic sacrifice. They simply:

- Built a stable financial foundation
- Combined monthly and lump sum strategies
- Automated discipline
- Maintained balance
- Stayed consistent over time

Mortgage freedom becomes far more achievable when homeowners stop operating randomly and begin operating strategically.

Chapter 10

The Ultimate Mortgage Payoff Game Plan: Bringing Everything Together for Financial Freedom

Reaching the final stage of this series requires pulling together every concept, strategy, and mindset shift discussed in previous chapters into one unified system. Mortgage payoff is not a single tactic or isolated decision. It is the result of combining structure, discipline, timing, income strategy, behavioral awareness, and long-term financial planning into a cohesive approach. Most homeowners never achieve true financial freedom because they treat mortgage payoff as a collection of disconnected actions rather than a complete system. The ultimate game plan is about integration—turning multiple strategies into one intentional roadmap toward financial independence.

At its core, a successful mortgage payoff game plan is built on three pillars: cash flow control, strategic lump sum deployment, and long-term wealth reallocation. Each pillar plays a specific role. Cash flow control ensures stability and consistency in monthly progress. Lump sum deployment accelerates debt elimination during income spikes or unexpected financial gains. Wealth reallocation ensures that once the mortgage is eliminated, the freed cash flow is redirected into assets that continue building long-term financial strength.

Without all three pillars working together, the system becomes incomplete. Some homeowners focus only on monthly payments and ignore acceleration opportunities. Others rely only on occasional lump sums without consistent progress. Others eliminate debt but fail to build wealth afterward. The ultimate game plan integrates all phases of financial movement from beginning to end.

The first step in building a complete system is establishing financial clarity. Homeowners must understand their full financial picture, including income stability, monthly obligations, savings, debt structure, investment contributions, and long-term goals. Without clarity, decisions become reactive rather than strategic. Many individuals attempt mortgage payoff without fully understanding how their cash flow behaves across different months or seasons. This often leads to inconsistent results.

A strong game plan begins by stabilizing monthly cash flow. This includes ensuring that essential expenses, emergency savings contributions, and basic investing habits are all protected before aggressive mortgage acceleration begins. Stability is the foundation that allows long-term consistency without financial burnout. Homeowners who skip this step often experience setbacks when unexpected expenses arise.

Once stability is established, the next phase involves designing a structured monthly acceleration plan. This usually includes a fixed additional principal payment that is sustainable across all income conditions. The key principle here is consistency over intensity. A smaller monthly amount that is applied every month for years often produces stronger results than sporadic large payments followed by long gaps of inactivity.

After monthly structure is in place, homeowners then layer in strategic lump sum opportunities. These include bonuses, tax refunds, side income, commissions, business profits, inheritance money, or any irregular financial inflows. Instead of making emotional decisions each time money arrives, the game plan predetermines how these funds will be allocated. This removes uncertainty and increases discipline.

Without strategic intervention, borrowers simply follow the lender's amortization schedule. But when structured lump sum payments and consistent monthly acceleration are applied, the entire equation shifts. The borrower begins influencing the outcome rather than passively accepting it.

Another essential component of the ultimate game plan is prioritization. Not all financial actions should be treated equally. High-interest debt, emergency savings, retirement contributions, and mortgage acceleration must be evaluated in relation to each other. A well-designed system ensures that mortgage payoff does not come at the expense of financial security or long-term investing.

For example, a homeowner may decide to maintain a fully funded emergency reserve while still allocating 30–40% of all extra income toward mortgage principal. Another may prioritize employer retirement matching while still aggressively applying side income toward debt reduction. The goal is not perfection—it is balance that supports long-term sustainability.

Behavioral discipline is one of the most important elements of the entire system. Financial success is rarely limited by knowledge. It is limited by consistency. Many homeowners understand exactly what they should do but fail to execute over long periods. Emotional spending, inconsistent habits, lifestyle inflation, and lack of structure often undermine even the best intentions.

This is why automation becomes a powerful tool inside a mortgage payoff game plan. Automated transfers, scheduled extra payments, and predefined allocation percentages remove emotional friction from financial decisions. When money moves automatically toward long-term goals, discipline is no longer dependent on motivation alone.

Another key concept is momentum building. Mortgage payoff often feels slow at the beginning because balances are large and interest is heavily front-loaded. However, as principal decreases, the system begins to accelerate naturally. Each payment has a greater impact over time. As balances shrink, psychological motivation also increases, creating a reinforcing cycle of progress and discipline.

Homeowners who remain consistent during the early stages often experience the most dramatic acceleration later. This is because interest reduction compounds in their favor over time. Early discipline creates exponential long-term results.

The ultimate mortgage payoff game plan also includes emotional management. Debt is not only a financial burden—it is also a psychological one. Many homeowners experience stress, anxiety, or pressure simply knowing they owe large amounts of money over long periods. A structured plan reduces emotional uncertainty by transforming debt into a measurable and controllable process.

Instead of feeling overwhelmed by a 30-year timeline, homeowners begin viewing the mortgage as a system they can actively shorten. This shift in perception alone can dramatically improve confidence and decision-making.

Another important element is flexibility. Life does not remain constant. Income fluctuates, markets change, family needs evolve, and unexpected events occur. A rigid payoff plan often fails under real-world conditions. A strong game plan is flexible enough to adapt without breaking.

For example, during high-income years, homeowners may accelerate aggressively using bonuses and lump sums. During lower-income years, they may rely primarily on structured monthly payments while maintaining stability. Flexibility ensures the system remains sustainable across decades rather than collapsing under pressure.

One of the most powerful long-term outcomes of a complete mortgage payoff game plan is cash flow liberation. Once the mortgage is eliminated, the monthly payment becomes available for reinvestment. This shift transforms financial trajectory entirely. Instead of income being consumed by debt obligations, it begins flowing into wealth-building assets.

This transition represents the shift from debt reduction to wealth acceleration. Many homeowners never reach this stage because they lack a structured plan to get there efficiently. But when achieved, the results can be transformative.

The final stage of the game plan is post-mortgage wealth deployment. Without a clear strategy, freed cash flow is often absorbed into lifestyle inflation. However, when directed intentionally, it can create exponential wealth growth through investments, retirement contributions, real estate acquisitions, or business expansion.

The ultimate goal is not just to eliminate the mortgage—it is to ensure that the financial discipline used during the payoff journey continues afterward in a wealth-building context.

When all elements are combined—cash flow control, lump sum strategy, behavioral discipline, automation, flexibility, and post-payoff planning—the result is a complete financial system that not only eliminates debt but also builds long-term financial independence.

Mortgage freedom becomes not just an achievement, but a transition point into a higher level of financial control and opportunity.

The homeowners who succeed are not those who rely on luck or occasional effort. They are the ones who build systems that work consistently over time, regardless of emotional fluctuations or external conditions.

That is the essence of the ultimate mortgage payoff game plan.

The Complete Mortgage Payoff System in Action

Let's examine how a fully integrated mortgage payoff system can transform a long-term loan into accelerated financial freedom.

Mortgage Details

- Loan Amount: $650,000
- Interest Rate: 6.0% Fixed
- Term: 30 Years
- Monthly Payment (Principal & Interest): Approximately $3,898
- Total Interest Over Full Term: Approximately $754,000

Now we apply a complete mortgage payoff game plan.

Step 1: Monthly Structured Acceleration

Homeowner commits:

- $1,200 extra principal monthly

New monthly contribution:

- $5,098 total monthly mortgage payment

Step 2: Lump Sum Strategy

Annual allocations:

- $20,000 annual bonus toward principal
- $10,000 annual side income toward principal
- $5,000 tax refund toward principal

Total annual lump sums:

- $35,000 per year

Step 3: Combined Impact

Total Extra Annual Principal Payments

- Monthly extra: $14,400 per year
- Lump sums: $35,000 per year
- Total additional principal: $49,400 per year

Step 4: Outcome

Instead of 30 years:

Mortgage payoff timeline: approximately 10–12 years

Step 5: Interest Savings

Original interest:

- ~$754,000

New estimated interest:

- ~$220,000–$260,000

Estimated savings:

$490,000+ in interest saved

Step 6: Post-Payoff Wealth Scenario

Once mortgage is eliminated early:

Freed cash flow:

- $3,898 per month

If invested at 8% annual return for 15 years:

Potential future value:

$1.1 million to $1.4 million

Final Insight

This example demonstrates the full system in action:

- Monthly discipline creates consistency
- Lump sums create acceleration
- Combined strategy shortens timeline dramatically
- Post-payoff investing creates long-term wealth

The ultimate mortgage payoff game plan is not about one tactic.

It is about building a complete financial system that transforms income into freedom, debt into opportunity, and time into wealth.

Final Tips and Suggestions for Mortgage Freedom

Reaching mortgage freedom is not just a financial milestone–it is a structural shift in how your entire financial life operates. It changes how you think about money, how you make decisions, and how you design your future. But the difference between homeowners who successfully reach that finish line and those who stay stuck for decades often comes down to a few key principles applied consistently over time. This final chapter is designed to bring everything together into practical, grounded guidance that can help you stay on track, avoid common pitfalls, and build a system that actually works in real life.

The first and most important principle is this: mortgage freedom is a system, not a single action. Many homeowners think they will eventually "just pay it off early" when money feels right or when life gets easier. But in reality, mortgage elimination almost never happens by accident. It happens through repeated structure–monthly discipline, intentional lump sum decisions, and consistent financial awareness over time. The homeowners who succeed are not necessarily the ones who make the biggest single payment. They are the ones who build a repeatable pattern and stick with it even when life is busy, unpredictable, or expensive. One of the strongest habits you can develop is separating "extra money" from "lifestyle money." Most people treat bonuses, tax refunds, commissions, or side income as opportunities to upgrade their lifestyle. While there is nothing wrong with enjoying life, the difference between financial stagnation and financial freedom is often how you treat these irregular income moments. When you begin assigning a purpose to every unexpected dollar before it arrives, you remove emotional decision-making. You turn randomness into structure, and structure is what builds long-term results.

Another critical tip is to avoid perfection thinking. Many homeowners delay starting because they believe their payments are not large enough to matter. They think, "I'll start when I can do something big." But mortgage acceleration is not about intensity—it is about consistency. Even small extra payments, when applied regularly over time, create massive long-term reductions in interest and years off the loan. The system rewards consistency far more than occasional large effort followed by long gaps of inactivity.

You should also remember that timing matters more than most people realize. Early principal reductions have a much greater impact than later ones because of how interest compounds. The earlier you reduce your balance, the more future interest you eliminate permanently. This means waiting "until later" is one of the most expensive financial decisions a homeowner can make without realizing it. Even modest early action often outperforms large late action.

Another important suggestion is to always maintain a financial buffer while accelerating your mortgage. One of the most common mistakes people make is becoming overly aggressive and eliminating liquidity. Mortgage freedom should never come at the cost of financial vulnerability. You should always have emergency savings, stable cash flow, and protection against unexpected life events. A strong payoff strategy strengthens your life—it does not weaken your flexibility.

A balanced approach often works best. Many successful homeowners divide their strategy into three categories: stability, acceleration, and growth. Stability includes emergency savings and essential financial protection. Acceleration includes monthly extra payments and lump sum contributions toward the mortgage. Growth includes investing, retirement contributions, and long-term wealth building. When these three areas work together, you create a financial system that is both aggressive and sustainable.

Another key tip is to automate as much as possible. Human behavior is inconsistent, especially when emotions, stress, or unexpected expenses enter the picture. Automation removes decision fatigue. When extra principal payments, investment contributions, or percentage allocations are automated, you reduce reliance on motivation. Instead, you rely on systems. And systems are what produce long-term results.

You should also regularly track progress, but not obsessively. Mortgage payoff is a long-term journey, and many people lose motivation because they focus too much on short-term fluctuations. Instead, look at yearly or quarterly progress. Celebrate milestones such as reduced balance thresholds, years shaved off the loan, or total interest saved. These milestones reinforce discipline and help maintain emotional momentum over time.

One of the most powerful mental shifts you can make is learning to see your mortgage as a flexible timeline rather than a fixed contract. Most people mentally accept the 30-year schedule as unavoidable. But once you understand that every extra payment directly changes the timeline, you stop thinking like a passive borrower and start thinking like a strategic operator. You begin to realize that the bank's schedule is only the default—not your limitation.

Another important suggestion is to avoid comparison. Some people will be able to pay off their mortgage faster because they have higher income, business profits, or investment gains. Others will move slower but more consistently. Neither path is superior on its own. What matters is whether your strategy is improving your personal financial situation over time. Comparison often leads to discouragement, while consistency leads to results.

You should also remain flexible as your income evolves. Mortgage payoff strategies are not static. They should adjust based on life stages. Early in your career, you may focus more on growth and balance. During peak earning years, you may accelerate aggressively. Later in life, you may prioritize elimination and stability. A strong strategy adapts rather than remains rigid.

Another key principle is to always understand opportunity cost. Every dollar you direct toward your mortgage is a dollar not used elsewhere. That does not make it right or wrong—it simply makes it strategic. Some environments favor mortgage payoff more strongly, while others favor investing or business expansion. The best financial decisions are made when you evaluate multiple paths rather than defaulting to emotion or habit.

Most importantly, remember that mortgage freedom is not just about money—it is about options. When your largest monthly obligation disappears, your entire financial life changes. You gain flexibility in career decisions, investment choices, retirement timing, family support, and lifestyle design. You are no longer forced to maintain a certain income level just to survive. You begin operating from a position of choice rather than pressure.

This shift is what makes mortgage freedom so powerful. It is not simply about owning your home. It is about reclaiming control over your time, income, and future decisions. That is why even partial progress toward mortgage reduction can feel life-changing—because every step reduces dependency and increases freedom.

Finally, the most important suggestion of all is this: stay consistent long enough for compounding to work in your favor. Most financial strategies fail not because they are wrong, but because they are abandoned too early. Mortgage acceleration requires time. Early stages feel slow, but later stages accelerate rapidly. What begins as small progress eventually becomes significant financial transformation.

The homeowners who succeed are not always the ones who start the fastest. They are the ones who stay consistent the longest.

Mortgage freedom is built through:

- Small decisions repeated consistently
- Structured systems instead of emotional actions
- Balanced financial planning
- Long-term thinking over short-term satisfaction
- Discipline during ordinary months, not just extraordinary ones

If you follow these principles, the mortgage becomes not a lifelong burden—but a structured journey with a clear endpoint.

And once you reach that endpoint, you don't just eliminate a payment.

You unlock a completely new financial life.

www.ingramcontent.com/pod-product-compliance
Lightning Source LLC
La Vergne TN
LVHW040519210926
848480LV00007BA/1521